CANDLE IN THE WIND

Candle
in the
Wind

by *Aleksandr Solzhenitsyn*

translated by KEITH ARMES
in association with Arthur Hudgins
with an introduction
by Keith Armes

THE BODLEY HEAD
and
OXFORD UNIVERSITY PRESS
London 1973

Oxford University Press, Ely House, London W.1

GLASGOW   NEW YORK   TORONTO   MELBOURNE   WELLINGTON

CAPE TOWN   IBADAN   NAIROBI   DAR ES SALAAM   LUSAKA   ADDIS ABABA

DELHI   BOMBAY   CALCUTTA   MADRAS   KARACHI   LAHORE   DACCA

KUALA LUMPUR   SINGAPORE   HONG KONG   TOKYO

ISBN 0 19 211835 8
ISBN 0 37 010265 7
Library of Congress Catalog Card Number: 73-77712

The translation has been made from the Russian text
Svecha na vetru published originally in *Grani*, no. 71
(Frankfurt am Main: Possev-Verlag, 1969), and
subsequently in vol. V of Aleksandr Solzhenitsyn's
Sobranie sochineniy v shesti tomakh (*The Collected
Works in Six Volumes*) (Frankfurt am Main:
Possev-Verlag, 1970), and was first published by
The University of Minnesota Press 1973.
This edition first published by
The Bodley Head and Oxford University Press 1973.

Set in the United States of America and printed
lithographically in Great Britain by
W & J Mackay Limited, Chatham

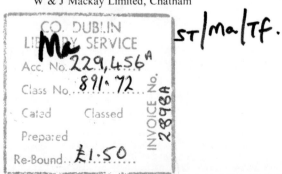

ACKNOWLEDGMENT

I am most grateful
to my colleague
Dr. Wassilij I. Alexeev
for advice during my work
on this translation.

KEITH ARMES

CONTENTS

CANDLE IN THE WIND
(*The light which is in thee*)

INTRODUCTION

by Keith Armes

Although it is Solzhenitsyn's novels that have brought him world fame, he has also written two plays, *The Greenhorn and the Camp-Whore* (*Olen' i šalašovka*)[1] and *Candle in the Wind* (*Sveča na vetru*) as well as a screenplay, *The Tanks Know the Truth* (*Znajut istinu tanki*). None of these works has been published or performed in the Soviet Union. The translation of *Candle in the Wind* into English is long overdue, for the play is yet another testimony to his faith in the human spirit and his concern for the future of mankind.

Solzhenitsyn has always been greatly interested in the theater: after graduating from secondary school in 1936 he applied to enter a drama institute in Rostov in order to train as an actor, but was rejected on medical grounds owing to a chronic throat ailment. It was not until 1954, soon after his release from the camps, that he wrote *The Greenhorn and the Camp-Whore*. It was accepted for production by the Moscow theater *Sovremennik* in 1962 only to be canceled after several rehearsals because of the political sensitivity of its theme. As is true of so much of Solzhenitsyn's work the play is largely autobiographical and reflects the author's experiences in one of the camps near Moscow in which he served the first year of his sentence for alleged anti-

1. Published in English under the title *The Love-Girl and the Innocent*, trans. Nicholas Bethell and David Burg (London: The Bodley Head; New York: Farrar, Straus and Giroux, 1969).

3

Soviet agitation and attempting to set up an anti-Soviet organization before being assigned to the "special prison" at Marfino (the *sharashka* of *The First Circle*).

Candle in the Wind was written in 1960 while Solzhenitsyn was working as a teacher of mathematics and physics at a secondary school in Ryazan'. It was initially accepted for production by the Vakhtangov Theater and the Komsomol Theater in Moscow, but was then rejected. Like *The First Circle*, which he was writing concurrently, *Candle in the Wind* reflects Solzhenitsyn's professional background as a mathematician and his interests in science and technology. However, whereas in *The First Circle* Solzhenitsyn is concerned with the misuse of scientific research under Stalin's totalitarian regime, in *Candle in the Wind* he deliberately chooses an unspecified international setting in order to express his fears about the consequences of an increasingly technological society for humanity in general.

Solzhenitsyn himself believes that the play is not a success, and it is apparent that as a stage production it does have its drawbacks, however important it may be as a vehicle for Solzhenitsyn's views. The first three scenes[2] introduce the personalities and attitudes of the principal characters and suggest the potential of "biocybernetics." The central issue is the persuasion of the heroine, Alda, by Alex to undergo the operation of "neurostabilization," but there is little real suspense: her submissive personality leaves no doubt that she will agree. The last three scenes demonstrate the effect of neurostabilization on Alda (the operation itself is not shown), as well as Alex's repentance for his terrible mistake. There is a secondary theme, the moral unacceptability of hedonism, which comes to a climax with the death of the old professor, Maurice. The appearance of the Craigs' poor relative, Aunt Christine, who reads from the Gos-

2. Solzhenitsyn does not subdivide the play into "Acts" and "Scenes," but refers to each section as a "Picture." However, I thought it best to use the normal English term "Scene" throughout.

4

pels over Maurice's dead body, relates the teachings of Christianity to Alex's faith in his conscience as a guide to conduct. The play ends on a predominantly pessimistic note: Alex fails to rescue Alda from the victorious biocyberneticists, for she, realizing the apparent inefficacy of Alex's beliefs, agrees to go to work for them. At the same time, however, Solzhenitsyn movingly stresses the importance of devotion and compassion and suggests that Alex will remain true to his ideals despite his isolation within an uncomprehending and hostile society.

Scene 4 (the celebration party) is crucial as an expression of Solzhenitsyn's philosophy. The ideological discussions, in which a significant character, an army general, participates, dominate the entire work. A Dostoevskian atmosphere (heightened by the sudden departure of Alda in a snowstorm) is created by the emotionally charged dialogue on the essence of human life and human society.

Solzhenitsyn does not attempt here, as he does in his novels, to achieve innovatory verbal effects by using archaisms or unusual prefixes and suffixes—techniques that have been the subject of so much controversy among Russian critics abroad. In general the language is appropriate to the milieu of the technological intelligentsia who dominate the play. Within this relatively neutral yet frequently colloquial language the recurrence of technical terminology drawn from cybernetics and computer science in and out of context intensifies one's awareness of the technocratic setting and emphasizes the themes of the play. Less successful, perhaps, is the literary flavor of much of the philosophical discussion, however suitable, indeed inevitable, it may be in elucidating the themes. In this translation I have tried to render the dialogue as accurately as possible in idiomatic English, since the play will be considered above all as a reflection of the author's views—and since Solzhenitsyn's detestation of inaccurate translation is well known. The preparation of an acting

5

version will no doubt involve cuts and stylistic changes in the dialogue.[3]

Noteworthy is Solzhenitsyn's use of music for dramatic effect, which reminds us of the symbolic use of music in *The First Circle* and *Cancer Ward*. While in *The Greenhorn and the Camp-Whore* Soviet songs are used with ironic intent and the repeated banging of a door increases the suspense which surrounds the hero's injury, in *Candle in the Wind* music and sound effects pervade the entire play and heighten emotional tension. Beethoven and Schubert, modern dance music and popular songs, are all drawn upon. He also makes symbolic use of the noise level of modern life, as in Scene 2 where the sonic booms of aircraft passing overhead and the thunder of nearby trains shatter Alda's equilibrium. Again, in the last scene the roar of the "superb engine" of Tillie's new car symbolically reinforces a major theme of the play.

Whether *Candle in the Wind* is successful on the stage will largely depend on how the principal roles are interpreted. The part of Maurice offers great possibilities as does the role of Tillie, Maurice's much younger wife, whose utter materialism and sexual aggressiveness are emphasized in the play. On the other hand, the hero and heroine, Alex and Alda, will not be easy to play in view of their relative colorlessness: here effective casting will be all-important.

Whatever its dramatic qualities, *Candle in the Wind* remains an exceptionally clear and comprehensive expression of Solzhenitsyn's views. Much of the play is autobiographical: Alex, a brilliant mathematician whose abilities had been greatly esteemed at the university, returns to freedom at the age of forty after having spent three years fighting at the front, nine years in prison, and five years in exile. In life the brilliant mathematician

3. I am grateful to David Ball of the Guthrie Theater, Minneapolis, for discussing technical aspects of the play with me.

Aleksandr Solzhenitsyn, recipient of a Stalin scholarship for university study, who was offered a graduate scholarship to work for a candidate's degree,[4] returned to liberty at the age of thirty-eight after three years at the front, eight years in labor camps, and over three years in exile. There is also an obvious correspondence between Alex's teaching mathematics at a school on the edge of a desert and Solzhenitsyn's own teaching at a remote school in Kazakhstan.

Alex's blessing the "necessary years" which he had spent in prison reflects Solzhenitsyn's own views about his fate. Similarly Nerzhin in *The First Circle* speaks of his gratitude to the *sharashka* for giving him the opportunity to think about himself and understand others, and Professor Chelnov in the same novel expresses the spiritual value of imprisonment in the memorable phrase, "Only a zek can be sure of having an immortal soul."[5] Alex's philosophy with its emphasis on the need for suffering and the primacy of the individual conscience is essentially Solzhenitsyn's own. The international setting of *Candle in the Wind* precludes, however, the introduction of other vital aspects of Solzhenitsyn's views. Although Alex refers to his service at the front with Philip, we do not find in the play any evocation of that idealism and comradeship of front officers so frequently expressed in Solzhenitsyn's novels, *The Greenhorn and the Camp-Whore* (in which it is a major theme), and—perhaps most movingly of all—his "miniature" *The Old Bucket. Candle in the Wind* inevitably also lacks the profound Russian patriotism that informs all Solzhenitsyn's work and constitutes the theme of some of the greatest episodes of *August 1914*. Nevertheless, the conversation in the play between the research assistants and Kabimba, the African who is writing a dissertation

4. The Soviet equivalent of a Ph.D.
5. Zek is camp slang for "concentration camp prisoner" (from z/k, the official abbreviation of *zakjučënnyj*).

at the biocybernetics laboratory, and Kabimba's decision to abandon his research and return home convey Solzhenitsyn's belief in patriotic duty and his rejection of the view that "homeland" (*rodina*) is an obsolete concept.

Solzhenitsyn has said of *Candle in the Wind* that he had tried to write a play remote from politics and outside any national milieu. "The action takes place in an unknown country at an unspecified period, and the heroes have international names. I did not do this in order to conceal my thought. I wanted to treat the moral problems of society in the developed countries, independently of whether they are capitalist or socialist."[6] Undeniably, however, Solzhenitsyn draws his material essentially from the Soviet Union—even though his views apply to all the "most advanced part of humanity" (to use his own words) and have universal validity for the future of human society.

The parallel between Alex's and Philip's ten-year sentences of imprisonment in "Desert Caledonia" as the result of a "legal error" and Soviet terror under Stalin is unmistakable. Similarly, Philip's concealment of his imprisonment suggests Colonel Yakonov's situation in *The First Circle* and Soviet sensitivity about the injustices of the past. Although Philip's espousal of the promising field of cybernetics has universal relevance, his enthusiasm for his profession and the emphasis on cybernetics throughout the play have a resonance for a Soviet audience which they could not possibly have in the West. Under Stalin cybernetics was declared a "bourgeois pseudoscience" (*lženauka*) and all study in the field was abandoned; therefore Soviet citizens associate the resumption of work in cybernetics with the changes in the intellectual climate since the death of Stalin. In the play the problems surrounding the development of cybernetics in the Soviet Union are brought to mind by Philip's remark about the "ter-

6. In an interview which he gave in March 1967 to the Slovak journalist Pavol Ličko.

8

rible battles" which he had to fight in order to create his laboratory.

Solzhenitsyn makes clear the target of his irony in Alex and Tillie's conversation about the magazine for which Tillie works:

ALEX

Glossy paper, color printing. I see it only deals with the problems of foreign countries.

TILLIE

Well, domestically everything's all right, so what is there to write about? ! But foreign problems, yes. We provide a survey of foreign countries, their economic defects and social evils. We play our part in the principal campaigns. We fight for peace, fight to ensure that the balance of power is always in our favor . . .

Later Tillie speaks about foreign propaganda:

Right now at the magazine we're in a rush preparing for a congress—the idea is that every country should have the right to have nuclear weapons, but we have to serve it up as part of the struggle for peace. It's a very subtle business![7]

When Tillie tells Maurice indignantly that one should always act in accordance with the "spirit of the age," we are immediately reminded of Rusanov's daughter, Avieta, in *Cancer Ward*, a cynical careerist who informs her father that one has to look at things flexibly and be responsive to the "requirements of the time."[8] Moreover, in *Candle in the Wind* the General expresses the same sentiments about the "rehabilitated" as does Avieta: ". . . what does the actual term 'rehabilitated' mean? After all it really can't mean that a person's completely innocent! Obviously he's done something, even if it's not very much." Significantly Solzhenitsyn pointed out in a discussion about *Cancer*

7. Tillie's reference to the "processing" (*obrabotka*) of the delegates could be understood either as "registration" or as "brain-washing."

8. Similarly, in *The First Circle* Yakonov tells Agniya, "You have to know how to distinguish in time what's new, those who can't fall hopelessly behind."

Ward held in November 1968 by the Prose Section of the Moscow Writers' Organization that "there is not one word of my own in Avieta."

Solzhenitsyn always devotes great attention to research before writing on any topic and the treatment of "biocybernetics" in the play suggests that he explored the scientific background extensively with cyberneticist friends. Possibly published work was also available to him. Little is known about Soviet research in the area (which is largely classified), but recent American research indicates that the questions raised by Solzhenitsyn in the play are by no means unrealistic.[9] "Biofeedback" techniques were originally developed for medical purposes to enable patients to control their own involuntary bodily functions by monitoring visual indicators of performance levels. These methods have been used to regulate heartbeat and to treat hypertension. Recent advances in electronics and computer technology, however, have expanded the use of biofeedback techniques far beyond purely medical applications. In particular, biofeedback has attracted wide attention as a means of inducing relaxation and as a legal means of inducing feelings of euphoria without using drugs.[10]

9. I am indebted to Patrick Davitt of the Management Information Systems Research Center of the University of Minnesota and Professor O. Frederick Kiel, director of the Center for Behavior Modification, Minneapolis, for information about American research on self-control of brain waves and involuntary bodily functions.

10. It is already possible to buy EEG (electroencephalograph) machines on which one can train oneself to achieve "alpha-wave highs." Moreover, voluntary alpha brain-wave training is currently being used in the United States to calm hyperactive children. For a discussion of recent American work in the area (from which the information above is taken), see Marvin Karlins and Lewis M. Andrews, *Biofeedback. Turning on the Power of Your Mind* (Philadelphia and New York: J. B. Lippincott, 1972). Collections of articles in the field of biofeedback can be found in J. Kamiya, et al., eds., *Biofeedback and Self-Control* (Chicago and New York: Aldine-Atherton, 1971) and in T. X. Barber, et al., eds., *Biofeedback and Self-Control 1970* (Chicago and New York: Aldine-Atherton, 1971). It is generally accepted that the Soviet Union is several years ahead of the United States in biofeedback research.

In *Candle in the Wind* Alda willingly undergoes "neurostabilization" because she is unable to cope with the stresses of everyday life. The treatment is only temporarily effective, since she is shocked out of her new equilibrium by the traumatic experience of her father's illness and death. Solzhenitsyn demonstrates, however, the danger to the human personality inherent in the inducement of relaxation by biofeedback techniques. The long-term use of such methods may easily lead to the individual's becoming permanently passive and escapist. Alda, in fact, loses the capacity for emotional experience and is reduced—as she herself says—to a "half-person." Even more frightening, she wishes to undergo "neurostabilization" again, for until she had been shocked out of her stabilization interval she had "felt so calm."

Solzhenitsyn is concerned about the larger implications of biofeedback techniques, or, to use the Soviet term, "biocybernetics." Clearly such methods could be used to regulate human behavior with or without the agreement of the people concerned in order to turn individuals into robots which operate only in accordance with predetermined norms. Solzhenitsyn's General, who had served earlier in the secret police, or "Department of Thoughts and Feelings" (referred to suggestively in the play by its three initials), realizes at once that the new science can be used to program a nation's population as machines. When the General[11] speaks of the possibility of carrying out "operations" on the brains of millions, we are reminded of the scientific antiutopias described by the Russian writer Evgeny Zamyatin in his novel *We* and by George Orwell in *1984*.

The danger of the misuse of power by a technocratic élite has long preoccupied Solzhenitsyn. The immediate hazard is that

11. Significantly, the General's views on the need to entrust the government exclusively to carefully selected and specially educated cadres correspond to the views of Stalin as described by Solzhenitsyn in chapter 19 of *The First Circle*. Earlier Stalin also referred to the importance of generalship and military genius.

11

self-seeking and unscrupulous scientists—such as Philip and Sinbar—will agree to put their talents at the service of a totalitarian state which stands ready to provide them with unlimited funds. In the play Solzhenitsyn exposes the way in which Philip rationalizes his careerism. Even Alex needs to make his "terrible mistake" with Alda before his conscience compels him to renounce research on "neurostabilization," whereas in *The First Circle* Nerzhin and Gerasimovich needed no such lesson before they refused to work on thought-control devices for Stalin.

The second danger is that a technocratic élite will use its power to create an "ideally regulated" society which will destroy human individuality. Solzhenitsyn rejects Terbolm's belief that science can complement man's conscience and his claim that with "social cybernetics" "there won't be any 'processing' of millions of people! Any onslaught on people's souls! All we want to do is to help people to foresee their social future. Not to lead humanity down false paths." Solzhenitsyn's target is the belief widely held in Soviet technocratic circles that an ideal society can be built on the cybernetic principles listed by Terbolm: "one hundred percent accurate information, coordination, and feedback." Terbolm's pyramidal model of a totalitarian society is appallingly inefficient because it lacks these features, particularly feedback. For Solzhenitsyn, however, Terbolm's "electronic Leviathan" of an ideally regulated society is just as unacceptable as Philip's neurostabilization, because both imply the ultimate destruction of the human soul. One of the gravest consequences of the worship of science which Alex excoriates in the play is the readiness it encourages in mankind to place its destiny in the hands of the technocratic élite.

Professor Maurice Craig stands in the play for another danger, one that is perhaps far more insidious. He and his wife, Tillie, represent the hedonistic materialism that in Solzhenitsyn's view pervades modern society. Maurice's gastronomy and Tillie's "mottled Burgundy" car symbolize this cult of the material just as General Makarygin's "tobacco altar" symbolizes the soullessness of the "new class" in *The First Circle*. The technocrats also share this attitude, but only in the case of Maurice is "that feeling of personal comfort and wellbeing when you don't want to raise a finger for anyone else" elevated into a philosophy of life. Maurice's realization before he dies that he has wasted his life demonstrates the truth of Alex's belief that man needs a philosophy which is valid for death.

Solzhenitsyn's hero endures the spiritual trials of wrongful imprisonment and then of guilt for the destruction of Alda, emerging unhappy and alone but with a knowledge possessed by no one else in the play except the despised Aunt Christine. Like Nerzhin in *The First Circle*, Alex had learned in prison that "suffering is a lever for the soul," and he returns to freedom cleansed of materialism and filled with faith in the essential nobility of man. In Alda he finds that spirituality which he prizes above all else. She lives in a society that tends to crush man's soul, one that desperately needs idealists and nonconformists, not stabilized automata. Yet Alex destroys her in the arrogant belief that he has a duty to make her personality conform better to this society. Without even the rationalistic justification of Philip or Terbolm, he takes it upon himself to interfere with the "most perfect thing on earth"—another human being.

Alex does this because his awareness of the "internal moral law" has now been blunted by the rationalism and materialism of his new environment. He ignores Aunt Christine's injunction to heed the "light which is in thee"—the original title of *Candle in the Wind*. In this play we find expressed perhaps more vividly than anywhere else in Solzhenitsyn's work his faith in the primacy of the individual conscience. Alex tells Sinbar, who like Philip denies the existence of anything immaterial, that we all possess an inborn moral law. Man's first duty on earth, Alex maintains, is to live in accordance with its promptings, which are determined by the principles of an absolute morality. All-pervasive in the play is the author's belief that in "our century of steel and the atom, of space, electric power, and cybernetics" it is especially difficult to heed what Alex calls that "stupid, in-born feeling."

The Tolstoyan claim that man's first responsibility is to his conscience is allied to the Tolstoyan call for "simplification."[12] Solzhenitsyn's rejection of the consumer society is absolute. "It's not a question of how much you earn, it's a question of how little you spend," remarks Alex. When he tells Maurice enthusiastically of the advantages of life in a remote settlement, inevitably we are reminded of Kostoglotov's description of his *aul* (village) in *Cancer Ward* which reflects the author's own experience of exile in Kazakhstan. Maurice is appalled that Alex had been obliged to use candles for lack of electricity, but Alex retorts:

> Did Plato have a battery? Did Mozart have 220 volts? In candlelight, Uncle, your heart opens up. And when you go outside you have the wind blowing from the steppes and the smell of wild herbs! Ooh-ooh-ooh! And if there's no electricity, when the moon rises over the desert the whole universe is flooded with moonlight! . . .

Here the value of "simplification" is associated with the recurrent image of a candle as a symbol of the human soul. The profound relationship between asceticism and spirituality is depicted most explicitly, however, in the role of Aunt Christine, who lives in extreme poverty: "Just a hut with an earth floor, the stove smokes, the roof leaks . . . It's difficult even to believe that in our day and age someone . . ." Impelled by mystical intuition,

12. Although Solzhenitsyn shares Tolstoy's detestation of luxury, he is far from accepting Tolstoy's views on culture or his idealization of the peasantry as a class.

the significantly named Christine appears at Maurice's deathbed, carrying a candle, in order to invoke Scriptural authority for the fundamental theme of the play—the need to abjure all that stunts the human soul.

For Solzhenitsyn it is frequently in old peasant women that true spirituality is found. Aunt Christine is reminiscent of Aunt Styofa in *Cancer Ward* who teaches the boy Dyoma to submit himself to God. But Christine recalls even more vividly Matryona in Solzhenitsyn's famous story "Matryona's Home"; unlike Christine she is far from being formally religious, yet she symbolizes the capacity of human spirituality to rise above egotism and greed. Christine's devotion to her cats conveys her readiness to help even the most feeble and defenseless creatures: the Kadmins' dog and the inhabitants of the municipal zoo in *Cancer Ward* illustrate Solzhenitsyn's tendency to see animals anthropomorphically. Like despised Matryona with her goat and her cat, lonely, ragged Aunt Christine redeems a world which devotes all its spiritual energies to accumulating material possessions. In the words with which Solzhenitsyn's autobiographical narrator concludes "Matryona's Home":

> We all lived beside her and did not understand that she was that very righteous person without whom, as the proverb has it, the village cannot stand.
> Nor the town.
> Nor our entire land.

In *August 1914* Solzhenitsyn evokes the profound spirituality of pre-Petrine Russia and medieval Europe to emphasize that man's duty to heed his conscience demands unceasing concentration on the light within him. "Man is called upon to perfect the structure of his soul," says the "astrologer" Varsonof'ev, implying that this spiritual obligation must be fulfilled even at the cost of indifference to grandiose projects for the reform of human institutions. We can merely guess at the laws of society, for it is an irrational, organic growth which can be tampered with only at great peril to its natural structure and historical continuity.

Weak and isolated as he is, Alex perceives that it falls to him to defend the individual human spirit against the onslaught of the dehumanizing forces of Philip's biocybernetics and Terbolm's social cybernetics. But for Alex human individuality means not hedonism and ruthlessness, but selflessness and humility. Thus it is Alda who symbolizes the "flickering candle of our soul." Alda's fate and Alex's incapacity to defend her seem to convey a profound pessimism about the future of man in modern society.

Yet Alex in his apparent impotence never loses sight of the means of human regeneration. Over the body of Maurice, who has let the "den of happy people" destroy his soul, Christine proclaims the Christian faith which informs the play. This faith is the basis of the "absolute morality" that gives Alex the courage to oppose his irrationality to the logic of Philip and Terbolm. At the end of the play the internal moral law which Alex seeks to obey leaves him in no doubt about the course he must follow despite the overwhelming odds against him.

Solzhenitsyn has written in *A Reply to Three Students* that he believes in two related innate human feelings: a personal conscience which prompts man in his dealings with other individuals and a personal sense of justice which prompts him in his attitudes toward society. "Justice exists if there exist just a few who feel it," asserts Solzhenitsyn, and Alex, Alda, and Aunt Christine redeem their society just as Matryona redeemed her village and ultimately her nation.

In *Cancer Ward* Shulubin suggests that a Christian society may be "too much to ask for." Solzhenitsyn holds nevertheless that each individual bears a personal responsibility for his acts in

16

order to ensure that he is not the cause of injustice. Moreover, each one has the duty to strive gradually to improve his world. Alex's remarks to Kabimba in the play reflect the same belief as Arkhangorodsky's words in *August 1914* on the nature of true patriotism—"we must include ourselves in the patient process of history: work, persuade and move things little by little." In *Candle in the Wind* Solzhenitsyn attempts to persuade a reluctant world of the dangers of materialism and of the worship of science. In doing so he proclaims that Christian faith which was later to inspire the *Easter Procession* and the *Lenten Letter*.

THE PLAY

Dramatis Personae
(supplied by the translator)

ALEX CORIEL, 40, a mathematician

PROFESSOR MAURICE CRAIG, 70, Alex's uncle, a professor of music

TILLIE CRAIG, about 40, Maurice's wife; works for a foreign affairs magazine

ALDA CRAIG, Maurice's daughter by a former marriage; works in a television factory

JIM CRAIG, 19, son of Maurice and Tillie

AUNT CHRISTINE, an old woman, a poor relative of the Craigs

PHILIP RADAGISE, 40, head of a university biocybernetics laboratory

NIKA RADAGISE, Philip's paralyzed wife

SINBAR ATULF, medical doctor, a colleague of Philip Radagise

ANNIE BANIGGE, a young woman in charge of the biology section of the biocybernetics laboratory

KABIMBA, a central African working on a dissertation in the biocybernetics laboratory

FIRST, SECOND RESEARCH ASSISTANTS, working in the biocybernetics laboratory

A GIRL from the programming staff of the biocybernetics laboratory

TERBOLM, 34, a researcher in social cybernetics

AN ARMY GENERAL

SCENE ONE

A large, bright room with a door on each side. At the back there is an unimpeded view of the ocean on which sailboats and occasionally motorboats and waterskiers can be seen. It is a brilliant summer day and everything is flooded with sunlight.

In the room there is a gas stove and a refrigerator, chinaware ranged on racks and shelves, also a set of frying pans. Near the kitchen area is the dining table at which Maurice is standing in an apron. He is tall and well built with an imposing, almost completely bald head and wears a pince-nez.

Alex Coriel is sitting next to a record player, near to which there is a record cabinet. The room is filled with the gay music of the Rondo from Beethoven's Second Piano Concerto. Alex is keeping time to the rapid movement of the principal theme.

MAURICE

One of the main criteria for judging people's taste is cheese. What cheese do you prefer, Alex?

ALEX

(*still listening to the music, laughing gaily, and gesturing*) I'm no connoisseur, Uncle, they're all the same to me.

MAURICE

All the same? You really are a savage, then! (*walks closer to Alex*) Perhaps you . . .

ALEX

Uncle Maurice! Why is it I like old music but not modern

21

music? How would you define it — what is the difference between twentieth-century music and nineteenth-century music?

MAURICE

Maybe you can't tell what grind of coffee you're drinking either?

ALEX

Is it important?

MAURICE

(*roars with laughter and switches off the record player*) No, you really are a complete savage! !

ALEX

(*making a feeble attempt to switch the record player on again*) Uncle! Let me hear the rest of it.

MAURICE

Oh, I've heard it hundreds of times already. All right, I'll give you the whole box of records. (*finally stopping Alex from turning on the record player again*) At the age of forty you have to start living all over again.

ALEX

Yes. That's just what I'm going to do.

MAURICE

But are you starting the right way? You tend to come out with some strange statements. You and I ought to have a talk, a good unhurried talk . . . Well come here and sit down. Now I'm going to feed you to make up for all those fifteen years!

ALEX

It's eighteen if you include my war service — (*He walks over to the table.*)

MAURICE

Eighteen? ! Start with the eel — the pork chop should cook slowly so the natural juices are left in the meat.

ALEX

Uncle, honestly, I'm embarrassed! For my sake you're . . .
all this woman's work . . .

MAURICE

(*busily preparing the meal at the table, speaking in a serious tone*) Alex! this triangle you see here — refrigerator, stove, dining table — has become my favorite pastime. It began with my not trusting anyone else to make coffee, but gradually I learned how to carry out other operations and now I often cook for all three of us. An outsider cannot cook lovingly. It needs a lot of intelligence, tact in other words. In ninety-five cases out of a hundred, housewives don't prepare food, they ruin it, let me tell you that! And the thing is complicated further by the fact that cookbooks get terribly out of date. I have a subscription to the magazine *Gastronomic News*. It keeps up with the results of the latest medical research. Well, since you don't understand anything about it, just drink what you're given. To the beginning of your new life! (*He drinks.*) Take some of this salad. All the same I can't reconcile myself — why didn't you write even once in all those years?

ALEX

But what would I write to you about, Uncle? And why?

MAURICE

(*angrily*) Hell! What do you mean — why? If only to ask me to help you! After all, you had a rough time, didn't you?

ALEX

It was a legal error. The evidence against us was so strong that we couldn't refute it. My friend and I were arrested just after the war when we were still in the army, given ten years, and sent to Desert Caledonia. We served nine of the ten years there. We had a year left to serve when

23

they found the real murderer. We were freed and given an official apology — but who can give us back those nine years?

MAURICE

Lost years!

ALEX

No, not really lost. It's very complicated. Perhaps those years were necessary . . .

MAURICE

What do you mean — "necessary"? You mean you believe that it's *necessary* for a man to spend time in prison? To hell with all prisons!

ALEX

(*sighing*) No, it's not as simple as that. There are moments when I say, "God bless you, prison!"

MAURICE

Idiot! . . . A-ha! (*goes over to the stove*) Now the chop is just right to eat! When the juices are coming out of it! (*He serves the chop to Alex.*) Take some peas. But the main thing is to give yourself some of this sauce. There are only a few people on this continent who know the secret of this sauce. And I'm one of them.

ALEX

Uncle Maurice! That's enough. I'm trying to stop eating so much. Most of what we swallow does us no good at all.

MAURICE

Yes, yes . . . (*serving Alex with food*) You're beginning to show clear signs of mental unbalance. Food is one of the joys of life and you're trying to give it up! And according to you it does you no good! I thought you had really picked up some healthy ideas in prison. But now I'm disappointed. (*pouring wine into Alex's glass*) Drink! (*Alex drinks.*) Well, praise the wine, you scoundrel! . . .

24

ALEX

It's a really subtle wine.

MAURICE

I should say so! I got it from old Harff. It's been five years now since they freed you, hasn't it. Where were you?

ALEX

I stayed right there.

MAURICE

In Caledonia?

ALEX

Uh-huh. In a little house on the edge of a vast desert.

MAURICE

You didn't have enough money to leave?

ALEX

It wasn't the money. (*after a pause*) It was my beliefs.

MAURICE

And you still hold those same beliefs?

ALEX

Yes. Almost.

MAURICE

(*waving his arms*) You won't hold out! I mean against life! You won't hold out! (*He pours Alex some more wine.*) But there was a settlement, wasn't there?

ALEX

Yes, there was one. I taught in the school.

MAURICE

But for Heaven's sake! Probably there was no gas! Or running water! Or a sewage system! !

ALEX

(*laughing*) Of course there wasn't any gas! On the outskirts of the settlement there wasn't even any electricity.

25

MAURICE

No electricity?!! You were back in the Stone Age! What did
you use for light?

ALEX

Candles.

MAURICE

You can go blind like that!

ALEX

Did Plato have a battery? Did Mozart have 220 volts? In
candlelight, Uncle, your heart opens up. And when you go
outside you have the wind blowing from the steppes and
the smell of wild herbs! Ooh-ooh-ooh! And if there's no
electricity, when the moon rises over the desert the whole
universe is flooded with moonlight! — don't you remember
that, at least from when you were a child, Uncle? Why are
you blinking like that, all popeyed?

MAURICE

The moon? — How old are you? I envy you.
*Jim runs in, looking at the sea, away from Maurice and
Alex.*

JIM

Maury! Look, our neighbor has just bought a summer cottage here and he's already waterskiing! This is the third
summer we've spent here — can't you get me all the stuff
I need for waterskiing, Maury?

MAURICE

(*angrily*) Is that the way to talk to your father, you rascal?

JIM

(*noticing a stranger*) Sorry, I meant to say "Daddy."

MAURICE

Since I'm your father, you think you can pester me? A
yacht isn't enough for you? Or aqualungs?

JIM

(*with dignity*) It wasn't me who was asking for an argument, Daddy! But I am informing you with all due respect that I need everything for waterskiing. It's not in your own interest to compel me to look for the money myself.

MAURICE

What money, for God's sake? Where would you ever get the money from?

JIM

I'll find it. But my studies may suffer as a result.
He goes out.

MAURICE

(*so that Jim can hear*) Your work's already suffering badly, how could it get any worse? . . . Damn it, until he was six it was amusing to hear him call me Maury. But now you couldn't thrash it out of him with a whip. (*upset*) Why didn't you say anything? — Let me give you some coffee. (*serves Alex with coffee*) Do you have any money, Alex? You need some? Be frank. (*He pulls aside his apron and takes out his wallet.*) Can I give you a hundred or a hundred and fifty?

ALEX

No, no, Uncle, I have some. In fact, altogether I need very little.

MAURICE

What do you mean, you don't need any? Look how you're dressed.

ALEX

How I'm dressed? I don't have any holes.

MAURICE

Damn it all, you have the strangest ideas!

27

ALEX

But the coffee was really enjoyable. I hadn't drunk coffee
like that for a hundred years.

MAURICE

A-ha! That means you're not hopeless. Want another cup?
. . . You should buy all your coffee from Stilokhon and
make sure they grind it right in front of you.

ALEX

Tell me, Uncle Maurice . . . Where exactly . . . is your
daughter?

MAURICE

Alda? She lives here in town somewhere.

ALEX

What does she do?

MAURICE

To be frank, I don't know.

ALEX

Has it been so long since you've seen her?

MAURICE

N-no, why? Recently there was a celebration at the conservatory in honor of my seventieth birthday and she came.
There she was sitting at the end of the table. With such an
inspired look. I introduced her to everybody — they were
all surprised that I had a daughter. But I didn't get to talk
to her.

ALEX

So you don't see each other at all?

MAURICE

No, she used to visit me. After the war. After her mother's
death. She used to come and we couldn't have been more
affectionate to her. Tillie is fond of her. But Alda herself
somehow . . . keeps away.

ALEX

I remember her when she was still a schoolgirl — a delightful, lively little girl about fifteen. You haven't kept any photographs of her at that age?

MAURICE

There ought to be some, and they took a photograph of her at my birthday celebration as well. Wait though, I have the albums here at the cottage, I'll show them to you.

ALEX

I'd like very much to find her. But I couldn't get any information. She's probably not listed under your name?

MAURICE

I can't even tell you. She used to bear her husband's name.

ALEX

She's divorced?

MAURICE

The first husband's name. Then there was a second husband.

ALEX

I see . . . So now she's . . .

MAURICE

No, right now she's not married. But you're quite right, it's an abnormal situation: not to know anything about one's own daughter . . . I don't understand myself how it's turned out like that. If you find her be sure to bring her here!

ALEX

She dreamed of becoming a pianist. She didn't become one then?

MAURICE

She didn't become anything. If she did anything sensible in her life, it was to observe the traffic regulations, thanks to which she's survived. Anyway I was always against her music. What good was music to her? I wished her to have a happy, stable family life. But happiness is something you have to know how to fight for!

ALEX

I want to find Aunt Christine too. I've heard she lives in great poverty.

MAURICE

Is that right! — Christine as well. Funny woman, no doubt she's still alive too. Can she really still be alive? You just find her and tell me all about it. I'm tired of going on knowing nothing about my relatives, really I am. I'm so glad that you've turned up!

In the distance the intermittent noise of a car engine can be heard. The driveway is elevated so that one can see the top of a dark blue car driving up to the cottage. It stops abruptly amid sudden explosions from the exhaust and the engine is turned off. A slender, agile woman wearing coveralls for traveling leaps out of it like a ball hit by a racket, runs forward to the hood, and starts hitting it with a wrench.

TILLIE

Damned heap! (*She raises the hood and looks at the engine; shouts in the direction of the audience*) Dad! I want some grub! Got any meat? Fix it!

MAURICE

Pork chop?

TILLIE

OK, pork chop! (*She waves and shouts into the distance.*) Ji-i-im! Come here!

She sticks her head under the hood. Soon Jim runs up to her and they both fuss around trying to repair the engine, cursing and rattling tools.

30

MAURICE

    (*hurries over to the stove and puts something on to boil*)
That's Tillie. Of course, she won't recognize you. You've
scarcely ever seen each other.

ALEX

    I think I saw her just once, in Pink Canyon soon after Jim
was born. She was still hoping to return to the ballet.

MAURICE

    She didn't return to the ballet but she still dances at ama-
teur performances. Recently she fell in love with journal-
ism. Altogether, Tillie is a colorful, manysided personality.
(*frying something*) Yes . . . I got married three times in
my life, Alex — all three times to eighteen-year-old girls.
It consoles one somehow in one's old age.

TILLIE

    (*Leaving Jim to work on the engine alone, she enters the
room in her coveralls with a large wrench in her hand.*)
Maur! Right now I could eat a wild boar, fried! (*Noticing
the stranger she stops. Alex gets up from the table.*) Do
we have guests?

MAURICE

    No, he's a relative.

TILLIE

    A relative? (*coming closer*) Excuse my appearance . . .
But who is it?

MAURICE

    Your nephew.

TILLIE

    I didn't think I had such a grownup, nice-looking nephew
. . . But since you tell me he's my nephew — shouldn't
we at least kiss each other? (*throwing the wrench on the
floor*) I'm all covered in grease and dirt, you don't mind,
little nephew? (*They kiss.*) I'm so glad! I don't suppose

31

Daddy will be jealous if I kiss you once more? (*kisses him again*) But all the same, who is it?

MAURICE

Alex.

TILLIE

Alex? . . .

MAURICE

The son of my dead sister Margarita.

TILLIE

Ah, Margarita? . . . We met . . . ?

ALEX

At Pink Canyon, just before the war. (*Maurice is still frying something.*)

TILLIE

Ah, at Pink Canyon! So you were that brilliant student with a wonderful future who'd just graduated from the university, is that right? (*She makes movements of ecstatic joy.*) I'm so glad! We're so glad! ! (*She kisses him. Speaking rapidly*) Where were you? Where did you disappear to? Why didn't you write? Tell me! (*She moves back.*) You see what a workhorse I am! — I spent the morning at the editorial office and then I had to drive a hundred kilometers on the highway in this heat just so the family can live here and enjoy the ocean. On the way the engine started to give trouble and I had to mess around with it and crawl under it — I was lucky to make it back at all. (*She unbuttons her coveralls while speaking and steps out of them, revealing a colored dress. Jim starts the car.*) Well done, Jim! (*She throws her coveralls and the wrench in the direction of the front door.*) Pick them up, sonnie! (*She parades in front of Alex.*) Well, what do you think of me?

ALEX

You're lovely, Mrs. Craig.

TILLIE

That's all I need — "Mrs. Craig"! Soon you'll be calling me "auntie" or "grannie." Don't call me anything except "Tillie." (*again parading in front of Alex*) And how old am I?

ALEX

Nearly thirty?
Jim drives off.

TILLIE

(*roaring with laughter*) If it weren't for my son! But I'm a mother, Alex, do you understand, I'm a mother! (*She walks over to the table on which the record player stands.*) How do you like this table? It's delightful, don't you think?

ALEX

It's very elegant.

TILLIE

We only bought it recently. It cost sixty-five ducats. (*washing her hands*) I'm a mother, and the problem of having a nineteen-year-old son is putting wrinkles on my exquisite little forehead.

ALEX

I don't notice any wrinkles.

TILLIE

Ha! I know how to conceal them! It's a whole system I've got! It involves sleeping in cold fresh air, regular exercises, massage, an active life! If you want to keep a little girl's figure at the age of forty, you have to wo-ork for it! (*The chop is already on the table. Tillie sits down and starts eating quickly and greedily, meanwhile keeping up the conversation. Maurice serves her.*) Apart from all that, I have a motto — no doctors and only the most natural medicines and even then only in the very smallest doses!

33

ALEX

(*becoming animated*) That I can understand! That I'm in favor of!

TILLIE

Yes, I felt at once that we were going to see eye to eye! I treat Dad myself, you know. We have this book — (*she jumps up and gets a book*) *The Home Doctor*. What could be better for an educated person? Not to trust those indifferent, prejudiced big names, but to diagnose the disease oneself and select the treatment. For instance, what's wrong with Dad? (*leafing through the book*) He has the amentia syndrome. That means he has sick nerves. The symptoms are the following: emotional fluctuations and delusions. What delusions? He's jealous. If you weren't my own nephew, I would have got it in the neck for those couple of kisses. An African graduate student named Kabimba came to see a neighbor of ours who's his professor. And he and I simply went swimming together, just swimming, what's so serious about that?

MAURICE

(*stopping her*) Tillie — Tie!

TILLIE

Daddy! That's your racial prejudice! Why should an African be inferior to you? The twentieth century is the century of the equality of nations . . . We've worked out a regular diet in fact: Dad doesn't eat meat, I don't eat anything starchy, keep down on salty foods, regular evacuation of the bowels . . .

MAURICE

Constipation is a terrible business!

TILLIE

It's dreadful! So maybe you have to take a laxative in the evening, but then food is one of the joys of life! And here

34

is Professor Craig at the height of his creative powers, while
I . . .

MAURICE

Well, as far as I'm concerned . . .

TILLIE

What do you mean as far as you're concerned? You're seventy, but so far there's no sign of any illness you might die from.

MAURICE

My heart . . .

TILLIE

That's just autosuggestion! You're still vigorous, you cope well with the housework, you still have all your teeth. You know, Alex, recently Maurice had a birthday celebration — a little banquet that cost around two thousand ducats! Guests! Telegrams! From composers! From conductors!

MAURICE

Chew it properly! Chew it properly!

TILLIE

You're still perfectly capable of working, perfectly capable! All right, you've given up lecturing, but now is the time you really must write a new book.

MAURICE

How can I write a new book . . .

TILLIE

Well, at least republish one of your old ones!

MAURICE

Tillie — Tie, to do that I have to add some new ideas.

TILLIE

Then add some new ideas! Quite apart from the fact that with the furniture I've got the place looks like an antique shop, one goes mad with shame at having to drive around in that jalopy . . .

35

MAURICE

It's a sports car that's only two years old . . .

TILLIE

The design is com – pletely outdated! I'm consumed with desire to have the Super-88 convertible coupé in "mottled Burgundy" color, 315 horsepower! But Dad doesn't have the money!

ALEX

Well, you'll manage to get the money.

TILLIE

You tell us about yourself, tell us about yourself, why are we doing all the talking? Where do you work? How much do you make? Are you married? Do you have any children? . . . Oh, children, children! (*Jim runs along the driveway at the back, playing with a ball.*) My son's only nineteen and he's already beginning to play around with girls.

MAURICE

Some playing around when you have to pay for abortions.

TILLIE

But you wouldn't want to have that Mezia as a daughter-in-law? You ought to be glad that the lad at least has common sense. (*Jim starts listening to the conversation and walks over.*) But you're right, you're right! You must marry him off — without fail! And what you want is the simplest girl you can find from a low-class background — let's have less of all this education . . .

MAURICE

(*flaring up*) What's this nonsense? What do you mean — low-class background? . . .

JIM

What good to me will all her education be — can I use it to make soup?

36

TILLIE

We're absolutely lost without a woman around! We don't
have anybody to sew on buttons. We've even got moth
worms in the flour. You'll gradually get her trained and
then you'll be able to turn over the stove and the frying
pans to her.

JIM

What are you arguing for, Daddy? Who's going to get married, you or me? My mother is a farsighted woman, she
knows how to live.

TILLIE

We'll have an harmonious existence together. She'll be
crawling around the house with a rag dusting everything.

MAURICE

(*angrily*) What is this, you've already worked it all out together? Is that what we brought our son up for?

TILLIE

Maur! Take a tranquilizer and stop looking daggers at me!
I don't like it. Why do you find the idea of a low-class
daughter-in-law insulting? Don't you realize that our age
breathes democracy? One must act in accordance with the
spirit of the age! Personally, at the editorial office I always
understand the spirit of the age.

ALEX

What editorial office is that?

TILLIE

Algol magazine, have you heard of it?

ALEX

Is it a political magazine?

TILLIE

Well, it's sort of . . . an international review. (*She jumps
up and brings over a couple of brightly colored magazines.*)
Look!

ALEX

Algol — isn't that the name of star Beta in the constellation of Perseus, the one called the "Devil's Star"? (*He picks up the magazines and leafs through them.*)

TILLIE

Could be, could be, something like that. They don't pay much, but I don't do it for the money, I do it for the sake of my general culture and the intellectual life I get there . . .

MAURICE

Tillie couldn't stay at home and look after the house. She'd feel stifled.

TILLIE

I'd feel stifled! . . . I love *life,* Alex! I love life in all its manifestations! After all, we only live once! One shouldn't let oneself miss out on anything!

ALEX

(*continuing to leaf through the magazines*) Glossy paper, color printing. I see it only deals with the problems of foreign countries.

TILLIE

Well, domestically everything's all right, so what is there to write about? ! But foreign problems, yes. We provide a survey of foreign countries, their economic defects and social evils. We play our part in the principal campaigns. We fight for peace, fight to help ensure that the balance of power is always in our favor . . .

MAURICE

It's only thanks to the efforts of their magazine that we still manage somehow to preserve peace on our planet.

TILLIE

So much energy! So much expertise! We have such a constantly exciting atmosphere at the office! Interviews, staff meetings, proofreading . . . You can't imagine, Alex, how I'm just run off my feet and never have time for anything.

ALEX

"No time for anything"? That's the scourge of modern man. You have *no time*? — that means you are living wrongly. Stop living like that, or else you'll perish!

TILLIE

Bravo! Brilliantly expressed! Where did you get ideas like that?

MAURICE

Where do you think! In prison!

TILLIE

What?

MAURICE

It turns out he spent ten years in prison.

Tillie freezes in amazement.

ALEX

That's how I began to have time for everything and still do.

MAURICE

But now he's completely acquitted. It was a legal error.

TILLIE

A-ha, an error! A-ha, acquitted. That's good. Thank God, who doesn't exist. But you know what, Alex? I'm a candid person, and I'm going to tell you, whether you like it or not — you're a terrible egotist!

ALEX

In what way?

TILLIE

Because you deprived us of the chance to do a good deed! You needed help — and how glad we would have been to . . . oh-oh-oh! . . .

Philip Radagise, broad-shouldered and tanned, dressed in a

*white sports outfit, comes up the terrace steps accompanied
by Jim.*

PHILIP

(*stops without noticing Maurice and Alex*) Madam! I'm
holding you to your word! You said you had an outboard
motor you weren't using. And I have a motorboat shell.
We'll put them both together and then I'll be able to teach
your offspring how to waterski.
*Maurice takes off his apron. Alex stands up, staring in-
tently at Philip.*

JIM

Mom! What a smart idea! Of course!

PHILIP

If there are no further reactions or questions, I've come to
get the motor. I'm tired of having to ski with someone else's
boat. Only I'm (*looking at his watch*) short of time, let's
step on it! Professor, excuse me, I didn't see you! (*says
hello to Maurice, then suddenly stares at Alex*) What? ? !

ALEX

Phil!

PHILIP

Al! (*They rush to each other and embrace with great emotion. Fascinated, Tillie runs up to them. Maurice is mysti-
fied.*) Where did you come from? Where have you been?

ALEX

What are you doing here?

PHILIP

Me? My cottage is next door! Where have you come from?

ALEX

Maury is my uncle.

TILLIE

Gentlemen! How come you know each other?

She flutters around them. They have still not completely let go of each other.

PHILIP

How come? We've known each other for hundreds of years.

ALEX

We were at school together. We graduated from the university together. We (*failing to notice that Philip is signaling at him*) were drafted into the army and sent to the front together and . . .

PHILIP

. . . and it was only then that we got separated!

TILLIE

Listen, that's terrific! I served at the front too! I fought at the front! What sector were you in . . . ?

ALEX

Finally, together we . . .

PHILIP

. . . I lost track of Alex at the front and since then he's never come back to our town.

JIM

Mom, how about the outboard motor? Shall I go and get it?

TILLIE

If Mr. Radagise promises to teach you how to water-ski . . .

JIM

You too Mom!

TILLIE

I'm afraid I've left it too late, haven't I?

PHILIP

(*with a generous gesture*) You're superbly built! You can do it, you can do it!

TILLIE

Go get it!

Jim runs off.

PHILIP

Can I help? Can I give a hand?

TILLIE

We'll call you. Let me change first.

MAURICE

So how is it exactly? You've been friends for thirty years?

PHILIP

That's right!

MAURICE

Well, you certainly deserve an opportunity to have a talk without me. We can look at the albums afterwards, Alex. Tomorrow I've got to drive into town, you can go with me, hunt around in my study, and choose for yourself the records you want.

ALEX

Thank you, Uncle.

Maurice goes off to the right. He already walks like an old man. Tillie hurries after him and catches him.

TILLIE

(*quietly*) Maur! Wasn't that a bit hasty — what you said about your study?

MAURICE

What of it?

TILLIE

Well, in the first place you're promising him the records. In other words you're making it impossible for him to have a completely disinterested attitude towards us. And then — you have no idea what he might have picked up in prison. You've got manuscripts by Rakhmaninov, excu . . .

MAURICE

(*raising his voice*) How dare you . . .

TILLIE

Sh-sh-sh! It's precisely because we love him that we ought not to put such temptations in his way!

Maurice waves her away angrily and goes off to the right. Tillie looks at the two friends and then goes off to the left. Alex and Philip begin to talk more loudly. Alex tends to remain sitting while Philip walks up and down.

ALEX

Why is it you — why don't you talk about the time you spent in prison?

PHILIP

You're mad! No one knows about it! I've concealed it and canceled it all out!

ALEX

But why conceal it? If you turned out to be innocent . . .

PHILIP

Innocent! Prison casts a black shadow! "He who has once drunk prison soup"!

ALEX

I don't know. I'm not ashamed of the years I spent in prison. They were fruitful years . . .

PHILIP

Fruitful? How can you bring yourself to say that? They took a pair of shears — like for cutting sheet metal — and they sliced a piece out of our lives! Tender nerves! Crimson blood! Young flesh! You and I were hauling wheelbarrows in a stone quarry, breathing copper dust, while here they were tanning their white torsos on the beaches! No, Al, it's the other way around — we must *make up for lost time!* Make up for lost time with every ounce of our strength! (*shaking his fist*) We have to get a double

43

share, a triple share out of life! It's our right! You and I know about our past — and that's enough! What if we announce to everyone what happened? No one will understand. When I returned to the university, I was flabbergasted: dimwits and runts whom we wouldn't have thought of as human beings, people who used cribs to get through the exams — now they're right in the forefront, they're senior bachelors of science! You think that it's very difficult to get the senior bachelor's degree? It just takes a lot of drudgery, that's all. Why waste time talking about it? — Elinody is head of the oscillation department!

ALEX

(*staggered*) Elinody? ?

PHILIP

Yes indeed! And Irun Ziodor is lecturing on mathematical physics equations!

ALEX

(*amazed*) I – run Zio – dor? ! Mathematical physics? !

PHILIP

(*roaring with laughter*) See! Judge for yourself. In our institute! But wait, I've already begun to sort them out. I showed them how to work! I don't spare myself — and so the people around me start pulling their weight! It's a fascinating sport, smoking the stick-in-the-muds out of the little nests they've built for themselves with their obsolete theories! ! (*roaring with laughter*) Listen, all these five years since your acquittal — where have you been?

ALEX

I stayed there. In Caledonia.

PHILIP

You mean . . . it was all connected with . . . your looking for the meaning of life?

44

ALEX

I suppose you can put it like that. (*laughing*) Nine years weren't enough for me, I stayed to think things through to the end.

PHILIP

Uh-huh, I see . . . How much did you earn? What did you do?

ALEX

I was teaching.

PHILIP

Kids?

ALEX

Uh-huh.

PHILIP

You were simply wasting your life!

ALEX

At first I was quite content. But then . . . I began to understand that my teaching was partly a lie. I was stuffing them with theorems, draftsmanship, talk about Space. But I wasn't preparing them to be able to resist the heart-lessness and calculation they would meet with in life.

PHILIP

Listen, you remember the way I was before the war? A real softy, gutless, a self-styled philosopher — remember?

ALEX

Yes.

PHILIP

Well, that's the way you are now!

ALEX

(*laughing quietly*) The other thing was that, to be frank, I just got fed up. Year after year going through sections of a textbook, questioning the kids on them, then some

45

more out of the textbook, and then again questioning the kids one after the other. Your brain dries up on you.

PHILIP

You can't plug up a volcano with a handful of straw! What's happened to you — you must have lost even the most elementary self-esteem? ! . . . And you found yourself a wife of the same type?

ALEX

No. My wife was different.

PHILIP

In *that* place? But who could you find there?

ALEX

Yes, I would have been a bit embarrassed to bring her here. But the question no longer arises. She's gone.

PHILIP

Well done! You abandoned her!

ALEX

No, oddly enough it was she who . . .

PHILIP

She abandoned *you*? (*He roars with thunderous laughter, gesticulating broadly at the same time. Alex joins in.*) She abandoned you? ! (*They laugh even more loudly, Philip shakes all over, waving his arms.*) Listen, she was very wise! She did the right thing! (*Another fit of laughter. Philip wipes away his tears.*) *She* abandoned *you*? ! (*He calms down.*) Brilliant! But where are you living at the moment?

ALEX

Nowhere so far. I just arrived.

PHILIP

And *what* are you?

ALEX

Nothing so far. Just a job-hunter.

46

PHILIP

For a schoolteacher's job? ! (*fiercely*) Al! You're not yet beyond hope! Listen closely: over the last five years I've moved mountains here! I'm rising meteorically, meteorically! I chose biophysics. It turned out to be a brand new field. I defended my first dissertation and managed to push through — after terrible battles — the creation of a biocybernetics laboratory at the university. Now the lab's expanding, and I'm at the head of it. We're getting extremely interesting results! In a few months' time I'll be a doctor of science with the rank of professor.

ALEX

Phil! You remember the way I was before the war? A human bombshell!

PHILIP

Yes, yes! That's why I have faith in you!

ALEX

(*sadly*) Now you are like that . . . How astonishing. We've completely switched characters. We've switched our views on life.

PHILIP

You're going to throw yourself into science like a lion, I have no doubt about it! You are going to work with me. You'll repeat my career, only even more rapidly. Only stop shoving your prison sentence into everyone's face. Even the university rector mentioned you recently. Everyone will be glad to see you back! As for those who're not glad — just keep out of their way! ! You're a brilliant mathematician. The raging wind of cybernetics is filling our sails and driving us forward! ! Our ship is moving full speed ahead! Before it's too late — grasp the rope and climb on board, old pal! (*stretches out his hands to him*) Life is a struggle! !

47

ALEX

(*does not take Philip's hands, but embraces him*) Wonderful, my old friend, wonderful. I am grateful to you. And I am so happy that you have come to be like this. And what you propose excites me, of course: our old university! The path of glory under the same roof that saw our youth . . . But if you could answer just one question for me . . . one question . . . *What for?*

PHILIP

You mean . . . how do you mean — what for? What is science for in general?

ALEX

Yes. *What* is science *for?*

PHILIP

You must be pulling my leg? Where is the problem? It's all so elementary! Well, first of all, its devilishly interesting! It's supremely enjoyable, surely you . . .

ALEX

Well then? Is it just for yourself? Out of egotism?

PHILIP

But wasn't all the material wealth created by humanity created through science?

ALEX

But that's not an answer either. What do we want wealth for? Does wealth better a man? I haven't noticed it.

PHILIP

You've really seized on a word I used! Well, not wealth, but all the material goods we possess on our planet, our entire civilization, our entire culture — everything was created by science, everything!! What is there to argue about?

ALEX

We can argue about the fact that when we boast about the quantity of material goods we collectively produce, no one

48

mentions what their production costs us. The answer is frightening: our entire human intellect down to the last fraction is devoted to the production of material goods! All our spiritual forces down to the last drop! No, I'm wrong, there is still something left to enable us to crush one another.

PHILIP

You've clamped onto me like a tick. After all, the twentieth century without science wouldn't be the twentieth century any more. Science is its soul!

ALEX

Or do you mean its soullessness?

PHILIP

You shouldn't have doubts about it, but instead go down on your knees before it! You should worship science!

ALEX

"Oh, great science!" That's the same as saying, "Oh, we great minds!" or even more precisely, "Oh, great me!" People have worshiped fire, the moon, and wooden idols — but I'm afraid that worshiping an idol is not so pitiful as worshiping oneself.

PHILIP

You developed into a real obscurantist during your time in the desert! You mean we should worship dear little God? What's the point of this stupid, purposeless argument about whether to develop science or not? As if that depended on us! That's the same as asking whether we should continue to revolve around the sun or stop for a rest. It's something that's above our heads. At a time when you have to decide about your own future — whether you're going to make yourself go on reciting Pythagoras's theorem to school kids or maybe work as a waiter in a restaurant? I like very much to go to restaurants, it's my favorite form of relaxation, but I prefer to sit at the table. Nobody will pay you a penny for your philosophy. You have to earn something, don't you? This entire city spends its time making ducats! The entire country spends its time making ducats! There is nothing alive that can survive without ducats!

ALEX

Surely you don't mean . . . for the sake of ducats?

PHILIP

Nonsense! We live for science, we breathe science, but if in the process the money just gushes out, it's a pleasant sensation, believe me! But surely I don't have to try to prove to *you* that science is the light, the meaning, and the interest of life for people such as ourselves? To run through the second half of the twentieth century with the relay baton which Newton, Maxwell, and Einstein have held and then at the finish line to hand it on to the twenty-first century?

ALEX

(*His head droops.*) Philip! I have the feeling that we will not need to hand on the relay baton . . .

PHILIP

Nuclear war you mean? That's a phenomenon that unfortunately doesn't depend on scientists.

ALEX

It ought to depend on them more than on anyone else!
Maurice enters from the right, holding an open album.

MAURICE

Alex! I've found some old photographs of your mom and dad and of you as a child. I suppose you don't have any left? Come over here when you've finished.

ALEX

You have! Thanks, Uncle. But what about Alda?

MAURICE

It's strange, but I couldn't find a single shot of Alda. I just don't understand who could have taken them out of the

50

album. They were there inside.

Maurice goes out again.

ALEX

I have to go, the old man hunted for them specially.

PHILIP

Listen, I scarcely know this family, I first met them less than a month ago. What's going on here exactly? She (*pointing in the direction in which Tillie had gone out*) is thirty years younger than he. How did it happen?

ALEX

My uncle had the misfortune — or maybe the good fortune — to keep on falling for young women until all too late in his life. Here you have an . . . illustration of it. Uncle was an authority on musicology, he wrote quartets and sonatas himself too . . .

PHILIP

Why I asked — Madam Tillie, speaking as one old soldier to another, is just asking for it. She's a hell of a woman . . . Now, Al (*making Alex follow him, he points out his house to him*) that's my cottage next door. You're not going to leave here before you come over. And I will keep you under lock and key until I get your written agreement to work with me. Any questions?

ALEX

(*laughing quietly*) We'll talk about it, all right . . . But how about you? Are you married?

PHILIP

(*All the vitality goes out of his voice.*) Y-yes, I am. (*after a pause*) But it's as if I wasn't married at all any more . . . (*another pause*) I got married to Nika two years ago when she was still a student. And we had such a gay, happy time together. She even got me interested in sports. And then suddenly she fell ill. Something happened to her

51

spinal column. And as bad luck would have it, just when she was pregnant. We had to sacrifice the baby. At first they tried to reassure her that she would get better, and she used to be able to get up. But then it became less and less frequent. Now she's completely bedridden. She lies there and watches me waterskiing . . . You'll see her today. Well, come on, old convict, third-rate bandit! (*He pushes Alex in the back.*)

ALEX

Bandit yourself!

Alex goes out through the door on the right. Philip looks at his watch and sits down. Unnoticed by Philip, Tillie quietly comes out of her room wearing a robe, stops, and looks around. Untying the belt of her robe, she then returns to her room, only to come out again immediately afterwards dressed in a swimsuit.

TILLIE

(*loudly*) Philip! I'm naked! ! Don't turn round!

PHILIP

(*starts, turns abruptly, and slowly gets up*) Listen! . . . (*Tillie bashfully makes a defensive movement, but remains where she is standing.*) Listen! ! (*Philip moves toward her with long steps while Tillie slinks back into her room.*) How much longer are you going to keep doing this to me . . . ? (*He pursues her into her room.*)

CURTAIN

SCENE TWO

A small wood with widely spaced trees and two or three tree stumps. At the back one can see a road along which silently pass open trucks, covered trucks with trailers, dump trucks, mobile cranes, bulldozers, scrapers, and a variety of mobile construction machinery. The sun is frequently hidden by clouds so that the soft autumn light constantly varies. Alex and Alda are seen walking through the wood. Alex is carrying Alda's raincoat as well as his own. Unlike the previous scene he is now dressed with great care.

ALDA

(*throwing out her arms*) What a gorgeous little wood! How lovely the sun is! What feathery clouds! (*She takes off her hat, releasing her dark hair.*) Now I can really breathe freely! You know, today is the first time for a long while that nothing constricts me. Almost nothing . . .

ALEX

What's been constricting you?

ALDA

I'm always afraid that somewhere they're planning to do something bad to me, that some misfortune is awaiting me . . . As if someone wanted to take away from me . . .

ALEX

But what can you take away from someone who has nothing?

53

ALDA

Oh, there is always something! . . . But today is such a happy day! . . .

She pirouettes around. Suddenly a loud boom is heard from an aircraft as it passes through the sound barrier, followed by the piercing howl of the aircraft itself. Alda starts, cries out, and presses herself against the trunk of a tree.

ALEX

Those damned aircraft, I'm sick and tired of them . . .

ALDA

(*Acting quite differently from before. She now appears depressed, somehow even suddenly older, and on the point of collapse.*) Well, now you've seen the way Aunt Christine lives. Just a hut with an earth floor, the stove smokes, the roof leaks . . . It's difficult even to believe that in our day and age someone . . . (*There are tears in her voice.*)

ALEX

(*watching Alda with alarm*) Yes, the way she lives is really heroic. Only how many cats is it she has — nine or ten? It seems kind of a lot.

ALDA

Al, she doesn't collect them, they go to her themselves. And people leave cats with her which children have mutilated — cats which have been made to swallow pins, with their paws cut off, or deliberately burned with kerosene . . . And she takes pity on them. You remember that cat which lacked muscular coordination, the one that kept falling down and twitching its legs . . . (*She becomes lost in thought.*) That cat is the only thing in the world that's weaker than me. It's just like me . . . (*She weeps.*)

54

ALEX

Alda! Alda dear! Don't go on like that! Any thought that comes into your mind can make you . . .

ALDA

Can that really be the way you also used to live in that Caledonia of yours?

An electric train roars past quite close to them. Alda covers her ears and shrinks together until the train has passed.

ALEX

Me? ! Far better. True enough, my house was also built of clay and I had to bend down to get through the door, like this . . . (*He shows her.*) But inside I could stand up straight (*straightens up*) . . . in the middle, that is. (*He laughs. Alda starts to smile.*) And there were two windows on the sunny side of the house. No, *I* had a really luxurious life there! So long as I was alone. But then my wife appeared on the scene. She was absolutely tireless and she was ashamed of our hut! She was ambitious as well and demanded that I erect a palace with a slate roof! She demanded that I earn more too. And that I take her to the city and the big stores.

ALDA

Tell me, Al . . . Oh dear, what was it I wanted to ask you? (*agonizingly*) Oh dear, what did I want to ask?? Oh, how I hate to forget my thoughts like this! . . . Now I'm going to rack my brains trying to remember.

ALEX

(*looking at her forehead*) — Just be calm. You'll remember. It'll come back to you. You'll surely remember it.

ALDA

Go on talking about yourself.

55

ALEX

I'd already finished. After my release I wanted to live quietly and very simply and to marry a girl with a primitive nature, a nature in which people like to say there is truth, strength, and meaning. But it turned out that nowadays all these primitive natures think only of how best to grab and buy things and impress their neighbors . . .

ALDA

(*Very intently*) You mean that you could really marry someone without loving her?? (*Alex nods his head hesitatingly.*) You too! ? You as well? ? How dared you?

ALEX

Well, in the first place, Alda dear, there was no one else to choose from there.

ALDA

Then you shouldn't have done it! Shouldn't have done it at all! . . . (*swaying from side to side as if in pain*) There's no love any more! . . . Nowadays there is no love . . . Marriage is just one great big lie . . . So when she abandoned you, you simply . . . took out a cigarette and lit up, is that right?

ALEX

Alda dear! I understood then that I'm not capable of living that way, calculating every step I take — what exactly am I doing, what will it do for my family, what if my dependents were to suffer? To have to please someone, worry about someone, and let that determine my philosophy. I live only once and I want to act in accordance with absolute truth. My wife did a wise thing: she immediately found herself another husband who made good money . . .

56

ALDA

(*suddenly remembering*) That's it! Tell me, Al, so you believe there's no need to earn a lot?

ALEX

God forbid!

ALDA

But how then, for instance, can you dress fashionably?

ALEX

But why dress fashionably anyway? So as to look like everyone else, like identical castings off an assembly line? People are made different, why try to force yourself into a standard mold?

ALDA

Now that's completely absurd . . . You've simply got out of touch with real life and don't understand. How can anyone go around looking like a scarecrow?

ALEX

That's precisely the reason they think up different fashions, so you will try to earn every penny you can and not have a moment to think of anything else.

ALDA

Well, you've got to have new clothes, haven't you? And change your shoes?

ALEX

Shoes? You should wear them until the soles wear out. That's the logical thing.

ALDA

(*laughing*) You've gone mad, you're quite insane. And you've got to change your furniture too, the style is different now . . .

ALEX

Why change furniture? As long as the legs are still in one

piece — why change it? That's terrible, Alda, that's exactly the kind of argument I used to hear from my former wife. (*Again the boom and roar of an aircraft are heard. Alda starts and cowers.*) Why give up your best years, devote your best powers to making money, and then waste the money on trifles?

ALDA

(*drooping*) Those damned ducats! How tiring it is to earn them! I get spots in front of my eyes from that endless checking of television sets. I can't stand the sight of any more television sets!

ALEX

For fifteen years I didn't see a single television set — but even so I can't stand the sight of them. Where there used to be a real communion between souls, now . . .

An electric train roars past nearby, drowning his voice. Alda covers her ears with her hands.

ALDA

But I'm not capable of getting any other kind of job. I despise myself so much for my disorganized life. I studied music and also foreign languages, but I never learned how to do anything properly.

ALEX

But when last week you sat down at the piano in your father's study . . .

ALDA

Ah, but I wasn't really playing! . . . (*She becomes sad.*) I cannot play just like that. I need to play for someone. Would you like me to play for you?

ALEX

Yes! Please do.

ALDA

All the same you've got to have your own piano at home and practice four hours a day.

ALEX

I don't understand Uncle Maurice. His daughter inherited his own musical gifts! But he . . .

ALDA

Dad planned to buy me a piano. He met Mom several times and promised . . .

ALEX

. . . but he not only failed to help — he kept you from going to the conservatory!

ALDA

I didn't want to go myself, Al!

ALEX

Why not?

ALDA

In order not to compromise Dad by my being involved in music too . . . And he was also very afraid on my account of that artistic milieu. Those people who are so noble as long as they're playing a role. And finally that's just how it turned out. (*She droops again and remains silent, for a moment. Alex looks at her with alarm.*) No, don't say anything against him, my father is a good man, a very good man.

ALEX

He has moments of impulse when he's capable of being a magnificent person.

ALDA

(*brightening up*) Is that true? Yes, of course that's true! Of course, he treated Mom cruelly, but Mom too always used to say that he was a great and wonderful man.

ALEX

And what about Aunt Christine? Not even giving her a penny for twenty years? I'm going to tell him what's what! And it wasn't out of stinginess, it was just the result of that feeling of personal comfort and wellbeing when you don't want to raise a finger for anyone else. How about you! He doesn't see you for years — yet he's completely calm in his mind.

ALDA

You're wrong! It was my fault! It was I who didn't want to go to see him. The way things have turned out now, you've brought me back into the family, but otherwise why make him live a double life, remind him of the past with my presence? . . . I kept on not going to see him, but then when I heard about his birthday celebration — I went along on the sly. I sat right at the end of the table, hoping I wouldn't be noticed, and enjoyed seeing them do him honor. The students — the present generation of them — signed their names in paint on a barrel of wine and put the barrel right up on top of the table. Then they filled everyone's glass with a scoop on the end of a long, long handle! (*She laughs very animatedly.*)

ALEX

(*smoothing the hair on her forehead*) Now I can recognize you again! Now you're just like that delightful little schoolgirl whom I met just before the war. (*Alda looks at him mischievously.*) If only you were always like that!

ALDA

If only every day were as happy as this one!

ALEX

You haven't kept any photographs of yourself as you were then?

ALDA

I don't have any, but Dad should have some. Didn't he show you?

ALEX

(*absently*) — What? . . . Your dad? That girl I knew before the war stayed so firmly imprinted in my mind that I kept on thinking about you when I was serving at the front and later during the first years I spent in prison. I even wanted to write to you.

ALDA

So why didn't you write? Not even once.

ALEX

When I was at the front? You were still only a little girl. Or from Desert Caledonia? When I had another ten years to do?

ALDA

But if you'd written to me — my life might have turned out completely differently. (*Again there is a sonic boom followed by the roar of an aircraft. Alda starts and begins to sob.*) What is that? What is that? . . . (*She drops to the ground.*)

ALEX

Alda! Alda! (*He drops down beside her and holds her by the shoulders. Alda sobs hysterically and inconsolably.*)

ALDA

Why is life so cruel to me, Al? . . . Why live such a life? . . .

ALEX

(*He puts his arms around her. Speaking slowly and deliberately*) No, this is impossible. You cannot go on much longer like this. I thought that you would be able to smile through this one day at least! (*Alda continues to sob.*)

61

Listen, Alda, little friend. You know I'm now working at the biocybernetics lab with my friend Philip Radagise. The way things have fortunately turned out, everything's ready for doing what you need, in other words for making a fragile person into an unbending one. You hear me? (*Alda falls silent.*) Giving to a person a stable, serene character and mental imperturbability. You're not ill and you don't need treatment in the normal sense, but you are too sensitive and vulnerable. You need to be helped to live. I'm already finding my feet in this new field and can appreciate its value. (*Alda raises her head and listens.*) Alda dear, let's try it! Give me your hand to show you agree! It's for your sake! So that a tranquil smile should never leave your face. You've had enough suffering, haven't you? (*Alda smiles feebly.*)

CURTAIN

SCENE THREE

A laboratory with three doors and a large window. Near operating apparatus is a desk, a drawer of which is open.

The two student research assistants, wearing dark lab coats, are bending over the drawer. The First Research Assistant is whistling a modern dance tune, shaking his body to the beat.

It is a dull day and the electric light is on.

SECOND RESEARCH ASSISTANT

That'll cost you a valuable piece.

FIRST RESEARCH ASSISTANT

It's worth two pawns. (*making a move on the chessboard hidden in the drawer*)

SECOND RESEARCH ASSISTANT

One pawn? (*making a move*)

FIRST RESEARCH ASSISTANT

No, two! (*making a move*)

Hearing a noise, they instantly close the drawer and bend over the desk. Annie Banigge enters through the center door: she is short and blondish, with a full figure. All her movements are decisive.

ANNIE

(*sternly*) Young men, what are you doing?

FIRST RESEARCH ASSISTANT

Taking down readings, Miss Banigge.

ANNIE

And what kind of curves are you getting?

SECOND RESEARCH ASSISTANT

Here you are. (*He takes a large sheet of paper from the desk and gives it to her.*)

ANNIE

(*looking at it*) Why do you only have readings for two values of the parameter?

SECOND RESEARCH ASSISTANT

How many should we have?

ANNIE

At least four. We need to have a family of curves. So get readings for the rest. (*She returns the paper, then goes to the door on the left, opens it, and shouts inside.*) Kabimba!

SECOND RESEARCH ASSISTANT

He went out, Miss Banigge.

Annie leaves by the center door.

FIRST RESEARCH ASSISTANT

(*follows her with enthusiastic eyes*) You know, I would ne – ever re – fuse!

SECOND RESEARCH ASSISTANT

(*opens the drawer again and sings while he considers his next move*)

— But Sinbar's girl

Is not ours for a twirl!

FIRST RESEARCH ASSISTANT

So now we need to have a family of curves — that's the equivalent of having to start all over again. After all, we're working for the boss himself, so let the boss tell us himself.

SECOND RESEARCH ASSISTANT

But the boss and Miss Banigge see eye to eye about every-thing, that's well known. (*He makes a move, then goes*

*over to the control panel, checks the dials, and regulates
the working of the apparatus.*)

FIRST RESEARCH ASSISTANT

(*Bent over the drawer, meditating his next move, he sings
a ditty, shaking and tapping in time with the rhythm.*)

— But Sinbar's girl is not ours for a twirl!

Sinbar the steamer's master . . .

In two moves you'll lose your castle!

*He suddenly closes the desk drawer. Kabimba, a tall
African, enters through the door on the right. The First
Research Assistant reopens the drawer and returns to con-
sidering his next move, while again whistling the same tune.
Kabimba looks sad. He walks over to the window, leans
against it, and looks out.*

SECOND RESEARCH ASSISTANT

(*still standing at the control panel*) Is it true that Sinbar
was never a sailor?

FIRST RESEARCH ASSISTANT

I asked too. No, he wasn't.

SECOND RESEARCH ASSISTANT

He's got just what it takes to be a captain out of Jules
Verne. (*He moves away from the apparatus.*) Kabimba,
Kabimba! Why are you so mournful?

KABIMBA

It's raining . . . (*looking out of the window*)

FIRST RESEARCH ASSISTANT

(*considering his move*) Smile, Kabimba! Show us your
pearly little teeth!

KABIMBA

I've received a letter from home. I should have gone back
a long time ago.

SECOND RESEARCH ASSISTANT

How long ago?

KABIMBA

After I graduated from the university, two years back. But the boss wanted me and I stayed. The deeper you get inside science, the difficulter* it is to tear yourself away.

SECOND RESEARCH ASSISTANT

What's bad about that, Kabimba? At least there is one genuine thing in life — science! And sport too.

FIRST RESEARCH ASSISTANT

When the referee doesn't cheat.

KABIMBA

Biocurrents! That's very interesting for everyone, but there's still oy-oy-oy so much that my country doesn't need. I should have gone back home with simple physics.

SECOND RESEARCH ASSISTANT

To organize the manufacture of ammeters for schools?

KABIMBA

(*emphatically*) Yes! My homeland is desperately poor, illiterate, and believes in me, while I sit here working on biocurrents.

FIRST RESEARCH ASSISTANT

(*after making his move*) That's comic, Kabimba! Homeland! (*laughing*) Where have you been all this time? People used to think in terms of their homeland in the seventeenth century or back around that period! But there haven't been any homelands for a long time now, they're a gruesome anachronism. Gruesome! There is only our little planet, and even that, it seems . . . (*He waves his hand hopelessly, then starts shaking his body again and smacking his lips to the tune of his earlier ditty.*)

SECOND RESEARCH ASSISTANT

(*after making another move*) Kabimba! I expect you're a member of some political party or other, aren't you?

* Kabimba's Russian is imperfect. (Translator.)

66

KABIMBA

Yes, the Liberal Democratic party.

Both the research assistants burst out laughing.

SECOND RESEARCH ASSISTANT

But who belongs to a party nowadays, Kabimba? Come to your senses! Liberals, democrats, progressives — all those gangs think only of themselves!

FIRST RESEARCH ASSISTANT

And everyone ought to think only of himself!

SECOND RESEARCH ASSISTANT

Give up that dirty business of politics, devote yourself to science! You're successful at it, you get results! (*to First Research Assistant*) Let's take a reading! (*He goes up to the control panel.*)

KABIMBA

(*angrily*) You're still just . . . children! You've got superficial impressions! You've never been anywhere outside this town, never seen anything, so don't try to start arguing!

FIRST RESEARCH ASSISTANT

(*still considering his next move, begins singing again*) Sinbar the steamer's master . . .

Quickly closes the desk drawer and turns toward the apparatus. Philip and Alex enter quickly through the door on the right. They walk toward the center door but stop on noticing the people in the laboratory. Philip looks gloomy and speaks very harshly.

PHILIP

What have you boys got? How many readings? (*He picks up the sheet of paper.*)

SECOND RESEARCH ASSISTANT

Three for each curve.

PHILIP

Poor. That's slow. No devotion to science. Really! And why do you have only two values of the parameter?

FIRST RESEARCH ASSISTANT

But you didn't tell us to . . .

PHILIP

Even if I didn't tell you, you could have realized it your-selves, you're not children. Four to five curves for the basic parameter — surely you could have figured that out? ! (*He tosses the paper back on the desk. The First Research Assistant catches it in time to stop it from falling on the floor.*) That way you'll never get anywhere! You need to *think*. And get away from moving at horse-and-buggy speeds. Tomorrow morning you start everything all over again. Right now you'll go and help Kabimba. (*The research assistants begin to switch off the apparatus and get their belongings together ready to leave.*) Kabimba! Are you ready to take human biocurrent readings today?

KABIMBA

Yes.

PHILIP

Go ahead then. We may begin any moment. (*Kabimba nods and goes out through the door on the left.*) Well, where's your cousin? (*He looks at his watch.*)

ALEX

Yes, I was wrong to rely on her. I should have gone to pick her up myself this morning. But without me the work here would have come to a stop. Alda is just like that, she may arrive an hour early . . .

PHILIP

But she hasn't.

ALEX

. . . or half a day late. She'll really hurry and be eager to be on time, but any chance encounter may throw her off.

PHILIP

To use our terminology — her free-run length is very short?

ALEX

Yes, the Brown element is very pronounced.

The research assistants have meantime gathered their belongings together, locked the desk drawer containing the chessboard, and changed into white lab coats. They leave through the door on the left.

PHILIP

But how are we going to be able to work with her then?

ALEX

That's just what makes her valuable to us! We're planning to vectorize her! — She can be as scatterbrained as she wants until the moment she undergoes the experiment. You'll be surprised yourself what an ideal subject she is for us! She thinks of something and then immediately forgets it. Or sometimes she listens to you, but somehow seems not to hear. She laughs, then suddenly starts crying. She's as confused and elusive as a reflection in the water.

PHILIP

Very interesting, we'll see. (*He lights a cigarette.*) Is she married?

ALEX

She's been married twice. Both her husbands . . . abandoned her.

PHILIP

Did they leave her with children?

ALEX

You know, she's so easily wounded, as soon as you make a careless remark, she starts crying — when she thinks of her

69

marriages she starts crying, so I'm afraid to ask. She lives alone, anyway.

PHILIP

Why doesn't she live with her father?

ALEX

With her father! Her father couldn't even manage to keep any of her pictures safely! All that's left in the album are two big marks like empty eye sockets. I went to see him yesterday and gave him a piece of my mind. We swore at each other and he threw me out.

PHILIP

I see. Just tell me: is the programming staff big enough for you?

ALEX

No! And it never will be big enough!

PHILIP

What do you suggest then?

ALEX

(*speaking quickly and confidently*) We need to change radically our entire approach. We need to design automatic programmers for every type of problem. To start with, our work load will be excessive, but then the new system will prove its value ten times over.

PHILIP

What about money? Personnel? Working space?

ALEX

We'll collaborate with others! There are lots of trained cyberneticists now.

PHILIP

You know, Al . . . I'm not too keen. When truth is discovered by someone else, it loses something of its attractiveness.

70

ALEX

    (*again speaking quickly*) Phil, you need to rise above that! If we have programmers coming between us and the computers — that's just horse-and-buggy cybernetics! This is my idea of how it should be: I think of something, and instantly the computer understands me! Or the computer thinks of something, and instantly I understand the computer. Just like that! That's why we need autoprogrammers.

PHILIP

    You're great. See how you've got into the swim of things. When before you were so doubtful.

ALEX

    (*very quickly*) I've made an effort, Phil, and I think I'm beginning to understand. It's not a question of my personal merit or of anyone else's. Right now in the whole of science we've entered into a period like that five centuries ago in geography: any half-baked ship's captain in a dilapidated schooner could set out to sea in any random direction and return having discovered a couple of new straits, if not a new archipelago! Now, just in the same way, in the sciences kids who are still wet behind the ears tackle problems which Rutherford would have kept away from and in three months' time they've already found the solution. It's as if some mysterious force had seized hold of us and . . . (*He notices that Philip is plunged into gloom.*) Listen, how about Nika? The doctors had their consultation?

PHILIP

    Yes.

ALEX

    Why don't you say anything?

PHILIP

    Ab – so – lute -- ly hope – less. Understand? During the

next few *years,* do you understand — years! — she will be completely bedridden. She'll just remain lying there, as she is now. And it's not impossible that one side will become weakened or even paralyzed. But despite all that her life is not in danger. She won't die. Nor will she live. She'll stay the way she is right now.

ALEX

(*taking Philip by the shoulders*) What is there to do, my old friend? What is there to do?

PHILIP

I well understand that to get a divorce in such a situation . . . is considered unethical . . .

ALEX

And then, Phil, medicine is developing at such a fantastic speed, there are new treat– . . .

PHILIP

No! I've inquired into everything! There's no work being done on anything of value. (*with a strained voice*) What a damned awful position to be in! And there are so many cases like that! When someone doesn't live himself, yet ruins someone else's life . . .

ALEX

Oh, but she's so young! She's scarcely lived at all yet! . . . She has such an imploring look in her eyes . . . Give her back her legs! Let her run around a bit!

PHILIP

I'm terribly, terribly sorry for her. But tell me — who had pity on *you* and *me*? We spent ten years at hard labor when we had done nothing — does that mean we're less deserving of sympathy than any other ordinary individual?

ALEX

I'm not sure. I'm afraid there's a boundary line that's easily crossed: we suffered innocently, so we're in the right, in

72

the right — but then suddenly we're in the wrong. In a moment, somehow, everything is reversed.

PHILIP

Come, come! Everything's reversed! Over those ten years I stored up in myself so much yearning, so much restrained energy! So what now? Surely I've earned joy in life? A full life? A child, finally?

ALEX

Well, you can live without a child.

PHILIP

What do you mean, without a child?

ALEX

Anyway children never grow up the way we want them to. They are born selfish and they live only for themselves. You should look for spiritual children.

PHILIP

But I already have a whole cartload of those — spiritual children. I want to have my own son, a dynastic son! Surely you feel like that too?

ALEX

No, somehow I don't . . .

PHILIP

You're just a degenerate, a pedant! You want me to wait! I'm forty years old, how can I wait any longer? Huh? Listen, Al, there is no life after death! We have only *one* life, *this* one! — and we must live it so we experience all its different colors.

ALEX

It's very difficult, Phil. We have only one life. But we have only one of something else too. And we will never be given a second one either.

PHILIP

What's that?

A stupid inborn feeling. A rudimentary one.

PHILIP

Yeh-yeh, old fellow, you'll have to come out with some-thing stronger than that. You mean conscience? — it's too im – mat – er – ial to live by in the twentieth century. We don't know its constituents. Its formula. Some people consider it to be simply a conditioned reflex. Conscience is a feeling that's optional. (*Annie and Sinbar enter through the center door. He has sideburns and is smoking a pipe.*) So now the entire fire brigade is present? Then we can hold a little conference. Sit down, friends! Let's think. Our lack of space is stifling us. We're short of people. We're even shorter of funds. Where can we get everything from?

SINBAR

The time has come to attack and destroy Terbolm. It's time to prove that all that social cybernetics is absolutely non-sense! But in any case we must grab his working space and his funds for ourselves.

ALEX

By the way, I didn't get everything you were saying. What exactly is this social cybernetics?

PHILIP

It's just ridiculous! They want to discover the *laws* of hu-man society! And then construct algorithms on the basis of these laws and use them to help along progress with the aid of a computer.

ALEX

Wait, that's quite interesting.

SINBAR

It's raving nonsense! We'll swallow Terbolm with one gulp. But even so that's not enough!

PHILIP

We've outgrown the limits of a university laboratory, we need now to become a separate institute.

ANNIE

(*She cannot take her eyes off her boss.*) Yes indeed! What vision!

Alex looks at his watch: he is evidently eager to leave.

PHILIP

But what about the people we need? Coriel proposes that we design autoprogrammers. Where do we get the people from?

ANNIE

It's precisely now while we're still part of it that we should make skillful use of the university. In the first place, there's the requirement that the students, including the mathematicians and the physicists, gain production experience. We should make them work for us! What do they spend their time doing? ! . . . Secondly, we've got the students' research papers. Various decrepit old professors dream up recondite topics. We ought to divide up our overall research program into different topics, get them approved by the administration, and then have the departments assign the topics to students!

PHILIP

In that way the most capable students will be drawn into our orbit. That's a brilliant idea, Annie! You're a real genius in science as well as in life!

ANNIE

(*very gratified*) I only reflect the light of others. But I'm a good reflector.

ALEX

OK, boss, I'm off, I can't stay.

PHILIP

(*calling after Alex*) Listen, why doesn't she come?
Alex goes off to the right.

SINBAR

(*smoking his pipe in an ostentatious manner*) All that's
just kids' stuff, boss. I didn't want to say anything while
Coriel was here, it's a sore point with him. But no private
company will give us the kind of funds we need. These
days only the state spends money in unlimited quantities.
If we could get ourselves attached to the Ministry of De-
fense or to the Ministry of Internal Security, then the Sen-
ate itself would look after our budget!

PHILIP

I understand that. I've thought about it. But if we get ourselves attached to a ministry, we'll lose our freedom to do
what research we want.

SINBAR

We won't lose a thing! We'll attach one or two programs
which are useful for them. But we'll continue to do what
we need to do. As a matter of fact I wanted to propose that
you meet someone interesting this very week. An officer
who has an important post wants to have a look at our
laboratory.

PHILIP

Is that right? . . . Well, friends, that looks like a solution?

ANNIE

And an excellent one!

PHILIP

It is a solution. A solution! Invite him, Sinbar. We'll have a
talk. So where are we now? Our experiments on animals
went off perfectly, so now we can begin on human beings.
If the individual Coriel promised us comes today after all
— we can still take her biopotential readings today.

ANNIE

On 200 channels?

PHILIP

Yes. Alpha, Beta, and Theta rhythms, all the acute waves and extraneous frequencies. After that . . .

SINBAR

. . . We make her lie down, so she's resting in the dark, then get her Delta rhythm readings. After that we'll use light flashes of constantly increasing frequency . . . Oh yes! Tell Kabimba that . . .

He gets up and quickly goes off to the right. Philip and Annie remain sitting, looking intently at each other. There is a pause.

ANNIE

All the same. I probably ought not to have gone to see you yesterday.

PHILIP

After all, you are a close colleague of mine. Why shouldn't you visit me?

ANNIE

It was a cruel thing to do.

PHILIP

But sometime we'll have to . . . start getting her used to it.

ANNIE

But the way she looked at me!

PHILIP

That's precisely what you'll have to learn to . . . get over.

ANNIE

I felt really vile . . .

PHILIP

But if anyone's to blame, let it be me. It's not your fault. If it weren't you, then sooner or later it would have been

77

somebody else. You have to look at these things realistically.

There is a pause. They look at each other.

ANNIE

All right. I'll try . . .

Sinbar enters rapidly.

PHILIP

(*getting up*) So then all the job assignments have been made. You'll call me. (*He stops as he is about to go through the center door. Absentmindedly*) There was something else I wanted to . . . Yes . . . Well, that's everything for the moment . . .

He goes out slowly.

ANNIE

Poor Radagise! Right at the moment of the greatest suspense, when he needs clarity and firmness of mind he has to have such a tragedy at home. (*Sinbar remains silent, gazing at Annie. Even when he is not smoking he continues to hold his pipe in his hands.*) Why are you staring at me like that?

SINBAR

(*standing solidly with his legs apart*) I'm waiting to see what else you're going to say.

ANNIE

I've said everything for now.

SINBAR

It seems to me you're not interested in what you ought to be interested in.

ANNIE

You mean our common cause?

SINBAR

I mean the boss's family affairs.

ANNIE

    To the extent that they affect his running the lab?

SINBAR

    (*going up to Annie and speaking more gently*) Annie! I think people are already whispering and laughing at our expense.

ANNIE

    It's always the woman who suffers the more from that.

SINBAR

    All right. I've understood. I've got the idea. It was my mistake.

ANNIE

    You don't know how many times I've cried all night.

SINBAR

    Well, now you're going to find an infinite variety of ways of reproaching me. (*He takes her by the elbows.*) Now I'm telling you: Let's get married! Get married at once! What do you . . . ?

ANNIE

    But I've been trained to think logically, Sinbar. You always used to say that we should wait till you'd finished your dissertation. So let's wait, there's even less time now.

SINBAR

    But until just recently you were insisting yourself!

ANNIE

    And you used to give me all that stuff about science, your old parents, your little sisters . . .

SINBAR

    Annie, you come from a comfortable background, you've always had an easy life. The moment you graduated I got you a job here. But I've known poverty, and it frightened me, and I don't want any more. (*He attempts to embrace her.*)

ANNIE

(*tearing herself away*) There are students around!

SINBAR

All right, so we wait then. But what's changed? For a whole month you haven't, haven't . . . Soon I'm going to go as wild as hell! You keep on thinking up various pretexts . . . I could suspect you . . .

ANNIE

(*emphatically*) It's never occurred to you that I've long had reason to suspect you . . . ?

They stand facing each other tensely, then relax when the door opens. Alda enters from the right wearing a raincoat showing traces of rain, followed by Alex.

ALEX

These are my colleagues. (*introducing everyone*) This is my cousin, Alda Craig — Anna Banigge, the head of the biology section of our laboratory.

ANNIE

Wow, how awkward and highfalutin, Mr. Coriel! (*to Alda*) Just call me Annie. (*They shake hands.*) I'll go and call the boss, he asked me to let him know at once . . .

She goes out through the center door.

ALEX

Dr. Sinbar Atulf.

SINBAR

(*shaking Alda's hand, speaking in a cold tone*) You're not a relative of Professor Craig's, are you?

ALDA

(*timidly*) I'm . . . his daughter . . .

SINBAR

What do you mean, he has a son, but no daughter.

ALEX

She's right in front of you, Sinbar.

80

SINBAR

No, there is some mistake. I know for sure that he has only a son.

ALDA

(*animatedly*) It's not Dad's fault, it's my fault! I lived on my own . . . (*Alex makes a sign to Sinbar and he goes out through the same door as Annie.*) Oh dear, people are going to think badly of Dad because of me! And you too! Even you insulted Dad deeply yesterday! But I will definitely reconcile you both again.

ALEX

Yes, of course you'll reconcile us. (*He helps her off with her raincoat and hangs it up.*)

ALDA

How sweet Annie is. Do you date her?

ALEX

I don't have the time right now for sweet girls, Alda. You realize how I'm just run off my feet here? I sleep five hours a day.

ALDA

Just watch out, or you'll lose your opportunity. (*looking around her*) Oh, why do I feel funny somehow? (*She looks around her again.*) Al, for some reason I feel afraid. (*She clings to him.*) Perhaps we'll cancel everything and go away, what's the point of all this.

ALEX

(*smiling*) I'm an "Al" and you're an "Al" too, what is it you're afraid of?

ALDA

I'm afraid even of you. You've become different since you came here. Tell me, will it be painful?

ALEX

Not a bit.

81

ALDA

But you haven't experienced it yourself?

ALEX

Having one's biocurrents read? Oh yes, they read the bio-currents of everyone who works in the lab and keep a record.

ALDA

Oh, well, all the same, Al, there's something inhuman about it. What's the point of it? Let's go!

ALEX

(*calming her and making her sit down*) Alda dear! But we agreed, didn't we. We discussed the whole thing. It'll be better for you. You don't have any choice. (*Annie, Philip, and Sinbar enter.*) This is Philip Radagise, the head of the laboratory.

Alda stands up.

PHILIP

We're glad to see you. Although you did . . . make us wait.

ALDA

(*hurriedly*) I can explain that! It just happened that way . . .

PHILIP

(*magnanimously*) Don't bother to explain anything. But . . . (*He looks at his watch. In the meantime Annie and Sinbar have put on white lab coats.*) and we'll go ahead without further delay. (*He also puts on a white lab coat.*)

ALDA

(*submissively*) Where do I go? (*Sinbar points to the door on the left. Lowering her head, Alda begins to walk toward it, but then suddenly stops.*) But excuse me, gentlemen, all the same I'm not just a guinea pig. Explain to me exactly what you are going to do to me.

Sinbar has already opened the door through which Ka-
bimba had gone out. He is wearing a white lab coat with
the sleeves rolled up. At a sign from Philip he closes the
door, remaining inside the room.

PHILIP

You have a right to know. Sit down. (*Alda sits down*
while everyone else remains standing. Alex stands behind
her chair while all the others, dressed in white lab coats,
stand facing her, watching her closely.) Well, first of all —
what exactly are biocurrents? Biocurrents are very small,
weak electric currents which flow constantly in every one
of our nerve cells. Everything we feel, think, experience, or
do is ultimately reflected in one way or another in our biocurrents or is determined by our biocurrents. We learned
to *read* biocurrents only very recently, in fact . . .

ANNIE

A year ago.

PHILIP

As far as our exercising a reverse influence on biocurrents
is concerned — that's precisely our aim at the moment.
First of all, of course, we're going to study your biocurrents
thoroughly, examine your encephalograms, and then with
the aid of computers we'll process . . .

ALEX

(*virtually whispering in Alda's ear*) All that's not for today, it's going to take many days.

ANNIE

Even weeks.

PHILIP

And then finally we'll subje– . . . we'll apply to you what
we call *cybernetic neurostabilization.* Stabilization! — that
means we will assure you of the absolute optimum . . .

83

ALEX

(*in Alda's ear*) . . . the very best . . .

PHILIP

. . . internal psychological state and we'll make it permanent, as if you had been born with it, as if it were not a gift of science, but a gift of nature. After that you'll no longer be afraid of any nervous shocks or blows of fate. You will never again experience terror or anger . . .

ALDA

(*jumping up and crying out*) Why are you all looking at me like that? ! I'm not mentally ill, am I? . . .
She groans and almost collapses. Alex catches her in time and he and Sinbar put her back in her chair. Annie brings her some water.

ALEX

Alda dear, calm yourself, whatever crossed your mind? . . . Drink some water. Alda, what did you imagine? You know that I'd never do anything to harm you.
Alda drinks some water and throws herself back in her chair. She is pale and lifeless.

PHILIP

Dear madam, all this is completely voluntary on your part, we are not compelling you to do anything at all, and you are free to go away. But finally, if you want us to, we can record someone else's biocurrents today while you watch, and you will be convinced . . .

ALDA

(*She sighs profoundly, then speaks feebly.*) You're not deceiving me? You won't lock me up in there? You won't leave me alone?

ALEX

Alda! !

84

ALDA

(*sadly*) What do you mean, "Alda"? It's easy to deceive me . . . (*She looks at everyone in turn.*) But no, I believe you. It was just a fancy that came into my head. What do I have to do? (*She stands up.*)

ANNIE

(*takes her arm and leads her off to the left*) Let's go, honey, we'll have to get changed.

They go off. When Alda reaches the door she turns around and smiles at Alex as if to forgive him.

ALEX

(*quietly*) Her excitement won't spoil the recording?

ANNIE

(*hearing Alex, speaking from the door*) On the contrary: the recording will be especially clear!

She goes out. Kabimba follows her and Alda.

SINBAR

It's very good that she's so excited!

He goes out through the same door, closing it behind him.

PHILIP

(*nodding*) It will permit us to determine with optimum accuracy her characteristic frequencies! Your cousin's just great, Al. She's just the person we want in order to obtain what we need!

ALEX

(*holding Philip back*) She's a little candle, Philip! She's a little flickering candle in our terrible wind! Perhaps I was wrong to bring her here? . . . Don't blow her out! Don't harm her!

PHILIP

We'll give her real granite-like mental health. We'll transform her nervous system into a nondeviating vector! (*stop-*

85

ping Alex from following him) Don't you go with us, you'll affect her. Don't go, stay here!

He goes out through the door on the left, closing it behind him. Alex, overcome by hesitation and repentance, moves first in the direction of one door, then the other. A girl from the programming staff enters.

GIRL

Mr. Coriel! The tape's been punched and it's ready to run!

ALEX

Oh yes? I'm coming . . . (*looking in one direction, then in the other*) I'm coming, I'm coming.

He slowly goes off after the girl through the door on the right. Near the door on the left a previously unnoticed illuminated panel lights up:

RECORDING IN PROGRESS
NO ENTRY!!

CURTAIN

SCENE FOUR

Radagise's house. The action takes place successively in a large drawing room with a grand piano, a record player, and a telephone; then in a small drawing room with a television set; and finally at the end of the scene in the hall. At the far end of both drawing rooms one can see into the dining room, where a lavish, festive table is already in disarray.

In the large drawing room a number of the guests are listening to Alda smoothly playing a work by Schubert on the piano.

In the dining room are about twenty-five guests, evidently university people, among them an energetic-looking middle-aged general.

In the small drawing room Terbolm is sitting while Alex stands listening to Alda play. Immediately after the curtain rises Alda finishes playing; the guests applaud and many of them cross over into the dining room.

ALEX

> (*obviously very disturbed, sitting down beside Terbolm*)
> Can that really be late Schubert? Can that really be late
> Schubert! ! (*He holds his head in his hands.*)
> *From the dining room Philip's voice is heard proposing an*
> *impromptu toast. Some of the guests are sitting, others*
> *standing.*

PHILIP'S VOICE

Dear friends! Many flattering toasts have been drunk today in honor of the founding of our new Institute of Bio-cybernetics, in honor of its fierce scientific battles, and in honor of the professorship granted to your obedient servant. But we have passed over one of the persons to whom we are principally indebted for our celebration today — Miss Alda Craig, whose de – light – ful performance we have all just applauded and whose kind cooperation with our laboratory over a period of many months has helped us to prove so brilliantly the effectiveness of our methods and our ability to transform the human personality. (*applause*) Before proposing my toast, however, I wish to hold up before you this brawny young man (*holding up a little boy with both hands; there is laughter because the little boy evidently wants to sleep*), Miss Alda's son, whom we have restored to his happy mother.

A VOICE

Radagise! You're so proud of him one would think you'd manufactured him completely in your biocybernetics lab. (*laughter*)

PHILIP

You can go on mocking as much as you want! We see in him the symbol of our success! (*Applause. He puts the boy down.*) So let's raise our glasses to Miss Craig and her son!

There is a loud murmur of approval. Everyone drinks.

ALEX

I didn't quite understand, Terbolm — how is it that you know the mistress of the house? You never visited Mrs. Radagise before, did you?

TERBOLM

Yes, it was at a hospital in Gran-Errol. I'm very well known there — I spent many years there on my back. I still go to see the doctors once in a while. And they once

took me to her bedside to encourage her with the example
of my recovery.

ALEX

Might I ask what was wrong with you?

TERBOLM

When I was young my legs were very weak. They're still
not strong even now. When I'm excited I find it difficult
to stand. I lay on my back for seven years. I wasn't sure
that I'd ever get up again.

ALEX

You lay on your back for seven years, you're now thirty-
four, how is it you've managed to achieve so much?

TERBOLM

You should be able to guess the answer from the analogy
with your own unhappy experience: I've achieved so much
precisely because I spent all that time on my back. The
lack of external movement stimulates *internal* movement.

ALEX

Nevertheless — what can have given you the idea of mount-
ing an attack on human society? !

TERBOLM

But isn't sociology *in general* — in other words empty
chatter — even more of an attack on society, when we attempt to interfere with the future without being able to
predict it exactly either in Time or in Space, or to calcu-
late precisely its shape and dimensions?

The General and Sinbar cross the stage.

THE GENERAL

Listen, doctor, we've already burned our fingers a bit over
cybernetics. Burned our fingers! Even such an extremely
useful branch of cybernetics as military cybernetics turned
out to have a highly tricky characteristic . . . uh-uh . . .
it used to overstep.

89

SINBAR

Overstep?

THE GENERAL

Yes! Overstep the tasks assigned to it by the command.

SINBAR

But that's initiative! You should be glad.

THE GENERAL

Listen, what is there to be glad of? Our first model was *antiair*. It was fed with radar information on approaching groups of aircraft and missiles, processed it all instantly, did a great job, and then automatically alerted the missile bases, airfields, and antiaircraft batteries — all ve – ery good!

SINBAR

Very good.

THE GENERAL

Not so good! We had doubts even then: uh-uh . . . what is the a-a-air command supposed to do? OK. Then they produced a second model for us — *air/water*. This model had information from submarines, ships, and torpedoes fed into it as well, all this data was processed, up popped the result, and the computer itself instantly came up with the optimum decisions as to which ships were to direct their fire where, what antitorpedoes were to be used, what mine-fields to be laid . . . But all our admirals . . . uh-uh-uh . . . You get it?

SINBAR

I'm beginning to catch on.

THE GENERAL

But then our electronic smart alecks started to make us a Supreme Staff Computer, plus a smaller one, a Corps Computer, plus an even smaller one, a Divisional Computer! And these models were going to have all the surface data

90

fed into them — the movements of motorized units, work performed by army engineers, river crossings, artillery positions . . . The computer processes all this information at a hell of a speed and comes up with a perfect optimum battle plan! ! See? See?

SINBAR

So we're guaranteed victory? ! Great!

THE GENERAL

But what the hell good is a victory like that to us? Who operates the computer? College kids! But what about the people who've had all the benefit of the experience of the world war and local colonial wars, people with chestfuls of decorations, great generals! ? What work in human society is valued more highly than gen – eral – ship! ? What geniuses have left a more profound trace in history than great gen – er – als? Alexander the Great, Genghis Khan, Batu, no point in listing them all. So what do you expect us to do with this cybernetics? S – smash it? !

SINBAR

But general! I assure you, sir, that biological cybernetics . . .

THE GENERAL

. . . won't we have to smash that too some time?

SINBAR

Maybe "smash" is the right word, except in a different sense; I mean — like in tennis — give it even greater speed! (*The General laughs loudly. A comic procession appears: the two research assistants, wearing turbans made of towels, march across the stage beating out a rhythm with a homemade tambourine and with a spoon against a pitcher. Next comes the Girl from the programming staff, performing melancholy dance movements. Last comes Kabimba, smiling sadly. All of the men have already had quite a lot to drink. Sinbar bars the way.*) What's all this?

FIRST RESEARCH ASSISTANT

A shadow has fallen upon our celebration, sir! On this gay evening we say good-bye to Kabimba and bury his dissertation . . .

KABIMBA

(*waving his hand despondently*) Take whatever you want . . .

SINBAR

But you'll come back to it again later?

KABIMBA

It'll all be obsolete by the time I get back to it.

SECOND RESEARCH ASSISTANT

Kabimba! It's still not too late to change your mind!

FIRST RESEARCH ASSISTANT

Kabimba! Don't pay for the ticket! The captain here (*pointing to Sinbar*) can drop you off in Africa for free!

GIRL FROM THE PROGRAMMING STAFF

Captain! Don't cut us up with your propellers! (*She pushes the students out of the way.*) Iron captain! We'll make way for you!

Sinbar and the General pass through between them. The young people then start up the procession again.

SINBAR

(*pointing out Terbolm to the General*) See that blondish guy over there — you know who that is? That's who you need to get rid of before he can do any harm. He . . . (*talks soundlessly to the General*)

TERBOLM

Right now reporters are besieging my two bare rooms, sniffing around, and hunting for information about where this computer is that's designed to represent the structure of the state. They ask me questions like can my computer stop a revolution, can my computer replace the government, can it guarantee successful universal disarmament? (*laughing*) But there is no computer. "What? Still no computer?" They go away disappointed.

ALEX

I'm afraid you shouldn't have published the article so early. Given away your ideas.

TERBOLM

What can one do? You can't let ideas just lie around unused. If we're not strong enough, let others build it. No one gives us any money. Nobody's willing to come and work for us. For instance, would you work for us?

ALEX

No, I wouldn't. But not because you don't have any money, but because I'm afraid you'll start carving up poor humanity.

TERBOLM

Coriel! That's forgivable from anyone else, but not from you. Why should we refuse the collective — society — the principles of information, coordination, and feedback which are possessed by every individual human organism and every collective of living cells?

Sinbar has meanwhile gone out.

THE GENERAL

(*walking up to Terbolm*) Couldn't you possibly replace the term "collective" by some other word? "Collective" somehow smacks of socialism.

TERBOLM

(*tries to get up, but sits down again*) It's not possible. It's the appropriate word. Let's take the brain. (*The room goes dark. A model of the human brain lights up: on a sphere one can see a great number of flickering points. The in-*

93

terior of the sphere is dark.) The cells are all connected together. (*Shining, living threads transecting the interior of the sphere begin to flash on and off.*) It is only thanks to these free connections that the organism is able to survive by successfully resisting external destructive forces and recovering from injury. If, on the other hand, the connections are subjected to strict control (*all the points and threads on the model freeze into immobility*) development is arrested and life itself is threatened. (*The model is switched off and the room lights come on again.*) In the same way human society has to be capable of withstanding the destructive forces to which it's exposed: droughts, epidemics, earthquakes, economic depressions, financial disasters, wars . . .

THE GENERAL

    . . . revolutions . . .

TERBOLM

It has to emerge from all this restored and capable of further development. But in order to do all this society needs nothing more than one hundred percent accurate information, coordination, and feedback.

THE GENERAL

But where does the computer come in?

TERBOLM

The computer works on the same principles of information, coordination, and feedback. The computer will be a model of society. And then you can take any reform proposed for society, and there will no longer be any need to discuss it in depth, make suppositions about it, or vote on it to try to decide whether it will strengthen society, or maybe weaken it or destroy it. We'll just program the reform, feed it into the computer, and in a few minutes we'll have the answer! !

94

ALEX

That's a great idea!

THE GENERAL

I don't get it at all! This idea of testing a reform on some kind of irresponsible computer when an authoritative decision can be made on it by parliament! or a minister! or, finally, by the council of ministers!

TERBOLM

The trouble is, you see, that people's actions can be influenced by transient moods, such as wounded self-esteem, group prejudices and antagonisms, vanity, or impetuousness.

ALEX

Why don't you come right out and say it — they can act out of mercenary self-interest! After all, isn't human society governed with the aid of man's evil motives?

THE GENERAL

(*staring fixedly at Alex, as he has repeatedly before*) What do you mean — what societies and when?

ALEX

Well, I meant earlier, earlier.

THE GENERAL

Oh, earlier? That's right. (*addressing Terbolm*) But what do you find wrong with modern democratic governments?

TERBOLM

Like in this model? (*The room goes dark. A model shaped like a pyramid lights up. At the bottom of the pyramid one sees a large number of small points shining with a steady brightness, but the number constantly decreases the higher the pyramid, while each point becomes proportionately larger. Lines connecting the top and the bottom of the pyramid also shine with a steady brightness.*) The model lacks flexibility. We have here a highly complicated

95

combination of elements. Curiously enough, we find nothing like it anywhere in nature. The organizational form you see here was invented by human beings and their efforts have proved a complete failure. Living cells prefer to combine together . . . (*the working model of the brain standing beside the pyramid lights up again*) like this. Without a master mind. (*The lights of both models go out.*)

THE GENERAL

Well, you know, gentlemen, we're all for democracy, but within reasonable limits. Without a strong hand democracy is impossible. What happens if this . . . collective of machines of yours goes mad and destroys the nation?

TERBOLM

There's inevitably danger in anything you design. A bridge can collapse or an airplane can disintegrate. It's the duty of the builders to eliminate the possibility of an accident.

ALEX

But in fact it's usually people who are guilty of abuses. In any case this computer won't try to accumulate capital or find cushy jobs for relatives! Or to consume more power than it's allotted according to its original design. It won't start a war and it won't demand territorial conquests.

THE GENERAL

I've been looking at you all this time but I just can't recall — haven't I seen your face somewhere before?

ALEX

I couldn't recall at first either. Didn't you serve earlier in the Department of Thoughts and Feelings?

THE GENERAL

Possibly.

ALEX

And didn't you once carry out an inspection of Desert Caledonia?

THE GENERAL

Yes.

ALEX

Well, I came to see you once. To make a protest on behalf of the convicts.

THE GENERAL

The *convicts*?!

ALEX

On account of the bad food and the bad treatment. However, my protest was in vain.

THE GENERAL

And you're not ashamed to refer openly to your having been there?

ALEX

As long as *you're* not ashamed! — *I* have been acquitted. Someone else turned out to be guilty of the murder I was accused of.

THE GENERAL

You know you really shouldn't flaunt your "acquittal" in everyone's face. You shouldn't interpret it to mean that you weren't guilty at all.

ALEX

But that's the way I do interpret it.

THE GENERAL

You're mistaken. (*addressing Terbolm*) Young man, what you just explained to us is some kind of maniacal folly. You want human society to be governed by computers?

TERBOLM

No, not at all! The computers will only model the reforms

and test them. While the computers will be governed by . . .

THE GENERAL

Engineers? Scientists? . . . Out of the question. Impossible. Listen! In order to govern society one has to be prepared from childhood. You can't be born into just any family and then govern. It's an ability which very few possess, unlike anything else. I advise you very strongly, young man, to choose a more . . . uh-uh . . . progressive field of activity. Try space research. Industry. Sport, if you like. And you'll have a most successful career. But as far as that machine is concerned, you won't get a cent for it anywhere. Maybe in the interests of democracy we'll even have to . . . tighten the screws on you a bit. (*walking off*) He wants computers to govern society! (*goes out of the room*)

TERBOLM

You see. And so no one is willing to come and work for me. And you're not, either.

ALEX

I'm afraid, Terbolm. Here we've taken just *one* human being — and what have we done? And you want us to take millions of people at once!

TERBOLM

But there won't be any "processing" of millions of people! Any onslaught on people's souls! All we want to do is to help people to foresee their social future. Not to lead humanity down false paths. (*Philip can be seen pushing a dumbwaiter with wine and plates of food in the direction of the small drawing room.*) We are only working out rules for the transition to an ideally regulated society.

ALEX

(*vehemently*) Oh-ho! "Ideally regulated" — that doesn't

98

necessarily mean ideal! For the individual! No, as far as I am concerned you . . .

PHILIP

(*loudly, gesticulating expansively*) My dear friends! This is immoral! You should know how to enjoy your leisure! *Enjoy your leisure! Otium post negotium!* Or how does the other phrase go?

TERBOLM

Otium reficit vires.

PHILIP

(*practically shouting*) Today we are *enjoying our leisure!* And you're talking shop? It's prohibited! (*He sits down on the arm of a chair in a free and easy manner.*) Listen, Terbolm, surely you're not still mad at me? Your field of research never interfered with mine! I don't care, you can push on with it till Kingdom come. But life is a struggle! There was a moment when we collided on a narrow path. But now the conflict's been settled. Let's drink to our friendship! (*He fills three glasses for Alex, Terbolm, and himself.*)

ALEX

But all these months Terbolm was made to . . .

PHILIP

(*laughing*) Yes, by the way, if it hadn't been for him (*nodding at Alex*) we would have finally smashed you, that's for sure. (*shouting*) But now the conflict's resolved! We're going to be independent of the university. They'll give you back your little budget, you'll get your work space back, you can even appropriate some of ours as well. There are no consequences whatever!

ALEX

The consequences are moral ones.

99

PHILIP

Al! What is not material is non – ex – ist – ent! Let's drink!

TERBOLM

For some reason social cybernetics gets under everybody's skin like mad. On social questions everybody considers himself an expert. I had a lot of enemies quite apart from you . . .

PHILIP

But I never was your enemy! And what are enemies to you? You have an even greater number of ideas! That article you published gave you a worldwide reputation! If we don't drink together this instant, I *will* be your enemy. You're a sociologist, I'm a biologist, I do the groundwork for you. Shall we drink to the groundwork? (*Annie comes up to them.*) In particular, you're offending Miss Annie.

TERBOLM

(*picking up his glass*) No, far be it from me to offend Miss Annie.

Meanwhile Alex drinks.

ANNIE

In all my life I've never had a greater reason to celebrate than today.

PHILIP

That's one thing. And the second thing is that Miss Annie has been so kind as to assume the role of lady of the house.

ANNIE

Only for today, of course . . .

PHILIP

And so you're offending her twice over.

100

TERBOLM

(*getting up in order to help Annie to a seat*) But then you must join us too . . .

ANNIE

Oh no! I have to be on the move the whole time and I need to have a particularly clear head today.

PHILIP

Oh, you can drink a little drop. (*He pours her a drink. Alex stretches out his hand in order to pour himself another drink.*) Hurry up and make up for lost time, Al! That's the way!

ALEX

What's the point of hurrying, Phil? The way it turns out, we haven't missed out on anything. Except maybe seeing medieval Gothic architecture.

PHILIP

That old junk! We'll pull all that down and build again from scratch with plastics and glass. And so let's drink to unity, to progress, to . . .

ALEX

But as far as possible without generals.

PHILIP

What do you have against the General? He's the friendliest person going! And well disposed toward us! Well, here goes, here goes, here goes! (*All four drink.*) Now we're all reconciled. Our conflict's disposed of! (*claps Alex on the shoulder*) Take it easy, take it easy, Al!

Philip goes off into the large drawing room. Annie starts to go into the dining room, but Sinbar, puffing his pipe, bars her way. After standing in her way for a moment, he finally moves to one side in a deliberately conspicuous manner. Annie walks past. Still smoking, Sinbar walks slowly around the small drawing room, examining the

101

*pictures on the walls. The sound of the record player can
be heard coming softly from the large drawing room.*

TERBOLM

And there she is right now, lying there with her eyes fixed
on the ceiling, right under the light bulbs, it's painful even
for her to turn over. And all of us here know about her
and keep on smiling at each other as if we didn't know.
That's the way things are in this world: it's our fate to be
happy together with others, but to suffer, be ill, and die
all alone. (*after a long pause*) Coriel! Seriously. Come and
join us.

ALEX

Quite frankly, Terbolm, I'm suspicious not only about
social cybernetics, but about all science in general. Science
has successfully proved that it's very good at serving the
cause of tyranny.

TERBOLM

(*thinks for a moment*) It's not science that gives birth to
tyrants. There were even more of them in unscientific
epochs and in unscientific countries.

ALEX

But science managed to give them good service too!

TERBOLM

It fell into unscrupulous hands! That's why we need to
create an ideally regulated society in which science is no
longer used for evil purposes.
*Sinbar switches on the television set. Both Alex and Ter-
bolm turn around. Alex makes an angry gesture.*

ALEX

Sinbar! Spare us! Don't turn the place into a madhouse!
*Sinbar switches off the television set and starts listening
to their conversation.*

102

TERBOLM

How about you? You are suspicious of science, yet you've made it your profession.

ALEX

Yes, maybe I will give it up, I don't know. The main question in life for me has always been: *Why*? After all if you think about every single minor action you take . . . Every time I go out of my house I always know where I'm going and why. When I buy anything, I always know why. But when it comes to an important action it's considered for some reason that you don't need to know or to think about it . . . Here I've been working for Radagise for the last six months and I keep on asking everybody: why are we doing all this? No one is able to give me an answer. Why do we need science at all? I get the answer that it's interesting, it's a process that cannot be halted, it's connected with the productive forces of the economy. But nevertheless — why? Everywhere we go we get one strange purpose or another foisted on us: we're supposed to work for the sake of work, or we're supposed to live for the sake of society.

SINBAR

That's a lofty and magnificent purpose. Why don't you like it?

ALEX

It may be magnificent, but it's not a *purpose*.

SINBAR

Why not?

ALEX

Because if I live for your sake and you live for my sake, we end up with a closed circle. That's still no answer to the question, "Why are we alive?"

103

But "why are we alive" is an inaccurate way of putting the question. After all we weren't born by an act of our own will with some preconceived intention. The question "*why?*" may be asked only either of God . . .

SINBAR

Now don't let's get dear little God mixed up in this!

TERBOLM

Religion's ridiculous, that's generally accepted. Then we could ask our parents.

ALEX

But we too are parents. So why do we give life?

TERBOLM

That's right. Or again: since you've already been born and have grown up as a conscious being, *what purpose* have you personally set yourself? Or do you have no purpose and live simply out of bitter necessity.

ALEX

Well, Sinbar? How about your purpose? And the purpose of your future children?

SINBAR

Happiness, of course, what a naïve question!

ALEX

All right, but what is *happiness*?

The scene shifts to the large drawing room, where most of the guests are to be found. The elderly guests can be seen at the back of the room playing cards. There is no sign of the little boy. Several couples, including Philip and Alda and the General and Annie, are dancing a modern dance to the music of a loud and shrill song on the record player. The dance soon ends and the General walks up to Philip and Alda while Annie walks across the drawing room, making sure that everyone is having a good time.

THE GENERAL

Thank you, professor, for an extremely enjoyable evening. I'll have to leave soon. Will you permit me in parting to ask a few questions of your ward?

PHILIP

Of course, General, of course!

THE GENERAL

(*to Alda*) I won't tire you? Or dishearten you?

ALDA

(*Everything she says this evening is spoken in a measured and indifferent manner, sometimes suggesting tiredness.*) Go ahead.

They sit down.

THE GENERAL

Tell me, did you use to experience the feeling of fear?

ALDA

Very much so.

THE GENERAL

You were *afraid,* right? And what exactly were you afraid of?

ALDA

It's hard for me to believe it now. I was afraid of everything. In the mornings I was afraid of having to go out onto the noisy streets. In the evenings I was afraid of loneliness, of the darkness.

THE GENERAL

(*with hope in his voice*) And now?

ALDA

I'm not afraid of anything.

THE GENERAL

(*throwing up his hands*) Magnificent! Wonderful! . . .
And how about, for instance, your fear for your son?

ALDA

Why should I be afraid for my son?

THE GENERAL

By the way, they took him away from you, didn't they?
By court order?

ALDA

No, my mother-in-law only threatened to apply for a court
order — and I gave in. I was at the end of my tether.
But now Mr. Radagise has gone to a lot of trouble to get
the medical certificates I needed, and I've resolutely taken
charge of him.

THE GENERAL

(*beaming*) *Resolutely*? That's interesting too. You used
to have . . . hesitations?

ALDA

(*laughing woodenly*) I never knew what to wear. Or how
to organize my day. Or what to fix to eat. If you'd given
me two identical pieces of candy to choose between — I
wouldn't have been able to choose.

THE GENERAL

That's wonderful! That's amazing! Well thank you, thank
you! You can't imagine how glad you make me! (*He gets
up. Philip also rises.*) Tell me, say if we take uh-uh
hundreds of people? Thousands? . . . Not yet going as
far as . . . uh-uh . . . millions? Could you carry out
operations on that scale?

PHILIP

Funds! All we need are the funds, General.

THE GENERAL

Then you have my guarantee! You can consider that as of

the current year your institute is already on our budget. (*He kisses Alda's hand. Annie has meanwhile walked up and is now standing beside them. Philip moves to see the General out.*) No, no, let me have the pleasure of being seen out by your charming hostess.

He says good-bye and goes out with Annie.

PHILIP

Where's your chubby little fellow got to?

ALDA

Annie's put him to bed somewhere. In Nika's room, I think. (*She nods to the left.*)

PHILIP

You've been very attentive to Nika, you've brightened up many of her evenings. Thank you. You understand, it was difficult to make up one's mind to do it, but . . . Her illness was so protracted . . . Here at home it was impossible to guarantee her proper care and all the necessary treatment.

ALDA

I can see that.

PHILIP

And I believe she'll be even better off there. She'll be given various courses of treatment . . . (*Alda nods.*) She'll begin to hope for a complete recovery.

ALDA

But there is no hope.

PHILIP

No. And what are you planning on doing now, Alda?

ALDA

I'm going back to my ordinary life.

PHILIP

If that means assembling television sets — I won't allow it! As soon as my institute expands I'll find you a job

107

with me. The pay will be better and also . . .

The telephone rings. Annie, who is now back in the room, picks up the receiver.

ANNIE

Professor Radagise's apartment . . . Yes, we're celebrating, but who is this? (*coldly*) Oh hello . . . Yes, this is Annie . . . Of course, everyone's here . . . I'll pass on your congratulations . . . She's here. I'll call her right away . . . (*loudly*) Alda! (*Someone temporarily turns up the volume on the record player, and Alda doesn't hear. Annie again speaks into the telephone.*) Why not? I'll call her at once . . . Hello! Hello! (*She looks puzzled. Putting down the receiver, she goes over to Philip and Alda.*) Excuse me, but Tillie Craig just called. She asked me to pass on her . . . most ardent, as she put it, congratulations to the new professor and the new institute. (*Philip is silent.*) Then she asked to speak to you, Alda, but hung up at once. Maybe you'll call her yourself? (*Alda shrugs her shoulders, gets up, and walks slowly over to the telephone. She sits down beside it and dials a number, but there is no answer.*) Phil! Soon I'm going to start being jealous of you — with Alda and Tillie as well.

PHILIP

(*smiling*) Sit down. (*Annie sits.*) You're behaving excellently today, with superb tact. You simply illuminate everything around you.

ANNIE

But don't think it's easy for me, Phil. In everybody's eyes I imagine I can see condemnation or mockery. It's my ambiguous position . . .

PHILIP

All right, so that it shouldn't be ambiguous any more, today you'll be the lady of the house right to the end. No more concealment! We'll close the door together after the last guest.

ANNIE

(*hastily*) Not yet!

PHILIP

Yes! ! How long do we living people have to stand aside because of a shadow? It's just not logical! It's bad enough that we couldn't even enter the house without experiencing this burden of reproach. But now she herself will come in time to understand everything and be reconciled to the situation.

ANNIE

Reconciled to what situation, Phil? To the fact that we are waiting for her to die?

PHILIP

But we're not waiting at all. Let her go on living. But we are going to live too!

The scene shifts again to the small drawing room. Terbolm, Alex, and Sinbar are in the midst of a lively dispute. Sinbar gestures with his pipe while arguing.

TERBOLM

So we accept that *happiness means mental fullness*? If you have the feeling that your life is completely full, then you are happy.

ALEX

That's close, but it's still not right. You can have the feeling that your life is completely full both for good and evil reasons. The life of a scientist is full. So is that of a lonely old woman who nurses sick cats. Also that of a scoundrel who enriches himself at the expense of others. Also that of a caterpillar eating away at a fruit tree. If all this is happiness, is that what one should make his goal? Shouldn't we distinguish between such different kinds of happiness?

SINBAR

But *who* is going to distinguish? You or I? Why should
the criterion of what is true happiness be your point of
view, and not mine or his?

ALEX

Neither mine nor yours! — it should be one's internal
moral law! One may be happy — but let it not be in con-
tradiction with that!

SINBAR

What is this internal moral law you're talking about? Innate, is that it? (*He roars with laughter.*) Go and study
medicine! There is simply no *organ* in our organism in
which an internal moral law could be located!

ALEX

I already know your theory: you explain the whole of man,
including Raphael and Chopin, by hormones.

SINBAR

Yes! Go and study hormonal life! And as for absolute morality — that's just a fairy tale! All truth is concrete! And
all morality is relative!

ALEX

That infernal pretext of the relativity of morality! You can
justify any villainy by the relativity of morality! But raping
a girl is always bad, in any society! Or beating up a child!
Or driving a mother out of her home! Or slandering others!
Or breaking a promise! Or abusing someone's trust!

SINBAR

Rubbish! Ut – ter non – sense!

ALEX

What do you mean? All that can be *good*?

SINBAR

How about killing your own parents when they're old? Is
that bad or good? Why don't you go and ask Kabimba?

110

There are tribes in which it's considered good, even humane.

TERBOLM

Well, perhaps there is a law, but it takes thousands of years before it becomes clear to us. And anyway it's programmed differently by every society.

SINBAR

Don't try to be obstinate! There is no absolute morality! Nor is there any internal moral law! And even if one did exist, there would be no force which could make us pay attention to it!

Alda enters unnoticed.

ALEX

There is such a force!

SINBAR

Name it!

ALEX

Death! ! The eternal mystery of death! The eternal barrier in our way — death! You can study cybernetics or the blue galaxies but all the same you can't overcome death!

SINBAR

A time will come when we'll overcome death as well!

ALEX

Never! Everything in the universe is mortal — even the stars! And we are *compelled* to construct our philosophy so that it should be valid for death! So that we should be ready for it.

SINBAR

I'm fed up with all this funereal moralizing! People use it to crush live, bubbling life! How long does the miserable business of death take — a bare moment of negation, a minor additional factor — compared to our long, varied, colorful life?

ALEX

Small in time, but not small in importance! Don't bother to hide — it'll find you!

TERBOLM

We talk about death as though someone else were going to die, not us.

SINBAR

We talk about death as though we were dying every day! The world is huge! There are three billion people in it. It's extremely unlikely that at any given moment, through this door (*he points to the door on the right*) — see, I turn fearlessly to face it — through this door should come anybody's death! (*Everyone turns around to face the door and waits for a moment. But no one comes in. Sinbar gives a short laugh. Alda comes up behind Alex and touches him on the arm. Alex turns around.*) And what is more, I'm going to go and look in the hall. (*looks in the hall on the right*) There's no one there either!

ALDA

Are you still arguing? Haven't you had enough? It's just depressing.

ALEX

(*Makes Alda sit down beside him. During the argument he had been happily excited, but now he has a gloomy air.*) What was it I wanted . . . Would you like to?

ALDA

Do you mean dance?

ALEX

What kind of a pastime do you call that — dancing?

SINBAR

(*Standing in the doorway, he talks across the room to Terbolm.*) I think I'll go and have a smoke at the open window outside.

He goes out through the door. Terbolm also gets up and goes off into the large drawing room.

ALDA

Why didn't you come and talk to me the whole evening? You could have told me how you liked my playing.

ALEX

Not bad at all. Technically excellent. How do you feel about it? (*He drinks.*)

ALDA

I think I did all right. Everybody liked it. (*Alex silently nods. Alda smiles.*) The General was just asking me a lot of questions. He was surprised. I hadn't told him before how I'd begun to take everything very calmly. Now I don't cry at the movies. Yesterday on the street I saw a bus run over a dog. A big red and white dog. It was crossing the street quite calmly at an angle and didn't see the bus. For some reason the bus driver didn't use his horn. The bus pushed the dog along a bit like something soft stuffed with cotton wool and then drove right over it. But you don't seem to be very pleased about my recovery, Al.

ALEX

What do you mean? I'm very pleased.

ALDA

After all it was you who wanted it more than anyone else.

ALEX

More than anyone else? . . . Yes, you're right.

ALDA

It was you who made me. Good for you! But now you're not pleased?

ALEX

I'm pleased, Alda. I'm pleased. It just seems to you that way because . . . well, maybe because . . . Doesn't it seem to you that you've changed towards me?

113

ALDA

Towards you? Maybe. I suppose you're right. But that too is for the better, Al. (*They look at each other.*) It's for the better. (*pause*) Oh yes, by the way, Tillie called me up just now, but she suddenly hung up.

ALEX

Perhaps something's happened?

ALDA

Why do you immediately assume it was something bad? *The hall. A clothes stand with winter overcoats and a large mirror: all the furniture is very ordinary. To the left is the door into the small drawing room: the front door is closed. Sinbar is standing smoking his pipe beside the small vent in the window. There is a brief ring at the door. Sinbar, irritated, glances at the door and goes unwillingly to open it, stepping back at once into the room. Tillie enters, dressed in a silver fur coat.*

TILLIE

You? ! You knew it was me?

SINBAR

My dear madam, when you work with biocurrents every day, like it or not, you start reading people's thoughts.

TILLIE

I'm . . . beginning to be afraid of you . . . However, did Annie tell you?

SINBAR

We haven't said a word to each other the entire evening.

TILLIE

Can I believe you? . . . How about your marriage to Annie, by the way? Is it being postponed?

SINBAR

Yes, I guess it is. So what?

114

TILLIE

One confidence deserves another. I'm not too sympathetic to this marriage.

SINBAR

Why not?

TILLIE

Well, it's an instinctive feeling. Women never know the reason for their antipathies . . . or . . . (*intently*) sympathies. Why don't you ask me to take off my coat?

SINBAR

I don't believe you want me to.

TILLIE

You guessed correctly . . . I came here in order to get to talk to you without being noticed, my friend. You are my friend, aren't you? You promised me your friendship!

SINBAR

Yes, I'm your friend.

TILLIE

Sinbar! I need male protection so much right now! Professor Craig's condition has seriously deteriorated; your prediction was right. After all I did to try to spare him! I tried all the time to stop him from going to bed and make him continue working right to the end! He was rewriting his textbook, but he never did finish.

SINBAR

As a treatment that's somewhat unusual.

TILLIE

But it's so obvious! I was afraid that a too serious treatment would give him too serious thoughts. If he'd stopped working, taken to his bed, and started thinking — that's exactly what might have hastened the end. But my method didn't help: the doctors say now that it's only a question of a few days. I'd like to have your telephone number. (*She holds out a notebook.*) I've got your office number, but I might need to call during the night, at any moment. (*Sinbar writes down the number.*) You realize his library is of enormous value, it's worth tens of thousands! There are manuscripts by great composers! Letters by Toscanini and Stravinsky! There'll be absolute bedlam in the house with dozens of people running around; the entire crew of his brazen relatives will turn up and they could swipe everything! We have to make sure that everything's sealed immediately. You won't desert me, Sinbar?

SINBAR

(*kissing her hand*) You're going right home then.

TILLIE

That's just it, I'm not! (*rapidly*) Right now at the magazine we're in a rush preparing for a congress — the idea is that every country should have the right to have nuclear weapons, but we have to serve it up as part of the struggle for peace. It's a very subtle business!

SINBAR

You'd be better off at home, Tillie.

TILLIE

(*She shudders and makes a pleading gesture.*) Well, tonight — it just can't be done! We're in a tremendous hurry to process the delegates! But from then on I'll be home all the time, I promise you. Oh, by the way, I have a new car! It's got pneumatic rear suspension, a hydraulic shift, the color is called "mottled Burgundy," and the interior is a real dream! ! — don't you want to come and have a look?

SINBAR

I hope I'm going to have a drive in it; right?

TILLIE

I hope so too! . . . And now can I ask you to do something for me: call Alda here for a minute.

116

SINBAR

All right. Only be careful with her. Mind you don't give her a shock. She's the product of four months' work on our part. Careful!

Making a warning gesture, he goes off left. Tillie inspects herself in the mirror, first with her fur coat fastened in front and then open. Kabimba, looking bored, enters from the left.

KABIMBA

(*stopping*) Oh-oh-oh-oh?

TILLIE

(*showing herself off to him with an animated movement*) I heard you're leaving! But you won't forget how we used to go swimming . . . ?

KABIMBA

It's difficult to forget you.

TILLIE

(*glances rapidly through the door*) There's no one there? (*pulling Kabimba farther away from the door*) Give me a farewell kiss, quick! A good strong one! (*She hangs on his neck, but jumps away almost at once.*) Tell me, Kabimba (*she sees Alda standing in the doorway*) . . . is it really true that your home is built on piles? That's terrible! In general — are you from northern Africa or southern Africa?

KABIMBA

Central.

TILLIE

(*waving her hand sadly*) Well, greetings to central Africa then! (*Kabimba goes off.*) Alda honey! Don't be frightened! (*in tears*) Daddy is *very* ill! He's a lot worse! Only don't get excited.

117

ALDA

(*making an abrupt movement and displaying strong emotion for the first time since the beginning of the evening*) Daddy? ! But he's — still alive?

TILLIE

So far, yes. So far he's still alive. I wouldn't have called you, excitement is bad for you, but Daddy wants very much to see you right away. (*Alda makes a move to go and get her coat but Tillie restrains her.*) This is such a dreadful time (*she wipes her tears away*) but I have work waiting for me at the magazine; I can't refuse. Oh, public duty! Go straight to Daddy. Jim's there already. And wait till I get there. But don't even think of taking Alex with you, that would kill Daddy! He mustn't get angry. I know — I'll give you a ride in my car. Get ready as quickly as possible! I'll wait downstairs.

She goes out. The scene shifts to the small drawing room, in which Alex and Kabimba are standing.

KABIMBA

. . . they're all rich and totally unconcerned, they'll never be able to understand how other people live! I hate myself for clinging to them! I hate them all!

ALEX

Kabimba! You know I've also fallen hopelessly behind them because of the time I spent in prison. So what am I to do now? Elbow them aside? Smash their windows? Kabimba! Hatred and resentment will never get you anywhere. They are the most barren feelings in the world. One has to rise above that and realize that we have lost centuries or decades — we've been insulted, humiliated, but that's no reason for revenge. Nor should we try. All the same we're richer than they are.

118

KABIMBA

(*indignantly*) We are? Richer in what way? In what way?

ALEX

Because we've suffered, Kabimba. Suffering is a lever for the growth of the soul. A contented person always has an impoverished soul. It's our job to build little by little.

Kabimba rubs his forehead agonizingly. Alda runs in, with her overcoat on, frantic with worry. Annie enters from the left.

ALDA

Annie! I beg you! Let my son spend the night here! Can he? Can he?

ANNIE

Yes, of course! But what's wrong?

ALDA

Oh, I just can't tell you! I just can't! Later! . . . Al! Come here! !

She pulls Alex out into the hall by his sleeve. Annie starts following them in alarm, but stops. The next scene takes place in the hall.

ALEX

What's wrong? (*The snowy wind blowing through the window vent tugs at Alda's scarf and he closes the vent.*) What's . . .

ALDA

(*extremely excited*) Daddy's very bad! Tillie's waiting for me downstairs! But don't you go!

ALEX

(*buttoning up her coat for her*) We quarreled, it's true. But if . . .

ALDA

What can be wrong with Daddy? ? I'm frightened! !

119

ALEX

> (*opening the door for her*) You . . . do please . . .
> Alda dear! Alda! . . .
>
> *They stand in the doorway. Alda reels toward him and he
> kisses her. Philip enters from the left. Without seeing
> Philip, Alex waves to Alda as she goes down the stairs.
> Her voice can still be heard from below. Alex closes the
> door and then notices Philip. The window vent blows open
> again and a snowy gust of wind rushes in. Philip closes the
> vent.*

PHILIP

> You know I've been meaning to tell you for a long time
> but I've been so infernally busy — why don't you marry
> Alda, old boy? She's as pretty as they come, where could
> you find anything better? As for her being your cousin —
> that's all nonsense, marry her!

ALEX

> That thought struck me a long time ago even without you,
> Phil. But I didn't know that . . . And I myself . . . And
> then it's all so complicated, so complicated . . .
>
> *Annie and Sinbar hurry in.*

ANNIE

> Chief! What have they done to Alda?

SINBAR

> Coriel! Where's Alda? You haven't let her go, have you?

PHILIP

> What? What's wrong with her?

ANNIE

> It seems to me she's been knocked completely out of her
> stabilization interval!

SINBAR

> If she goes over the maximum . . . !

120

PHILIP

How could you? . . . Al!

ALEX

I . . .

SINBAR AND ANNIE

(*advancing on Alex together*) Yes, how could you? After all our efforts! ! Four months! !

PHILIP, SINBAR, ANNIE

(*all advancing on Alex*) Our only example! The product of all our combined work! !

ALEX

(*outshouting them as he retreats*) Our! — combined! — work! — I take this opportunity of telling you — is now over! ! We took a marvel of nature and turned it into a stone! And I can already hear officers' boots stamping down the corridors! Permit me to be — free! !

CURTAIN

SCENE FIVE

Evening. Professor Craig's study. Two of the walls are covered with bookshelves. In the room are a set of library steps, a desk, two armchairs, a sofa, and an open record player on which lies a music score. Maurice is half-lying on the sofa with his legs wrapped in a plaid blanket. The door opens and Alda rapidly enters.

ALDA

Dad, Daddy!

MAURICE

(*raising himself up with difficulty to greet her*) Alda! ?

ALDA

What's wrong with you? Tillie informed me that you are very ill . . .

MAURICE

How glad I am that you've come! I couldn't have wished for anything better. Though who would come to see me now except for you? !

ALDA

Don't speak like that . . . You have so many friends, close friends. They love you and admire you enormously.

MAURICE

No, my daughter . . . Recently I've often thought that everything, everything I've done, was wrong — and felt

122

regret for the opportunities I missed. We rush to try to grab everything so as not to feel regret later. But the moment when it's terrible to feel regret is when one is dying . . . How should one live in order not to feel regret when one is dying? . . .

ALDA

Dad! Remember your birthday celebration! The number of your former pupils who were there! All the expressions of gratitude!

MAURICE

Those were all pupils I had long ago when I was still capable of something. And half of those aren't worth anything . . . I crammed terms and quotations into their heads, but not one iota of kind feeling. My life's been valueless . . . I've lived in this evil den of happy people — and it has swallowed me up . . . That's how my life's been wasted, the life everyone calls a happy one . . . But why is it that we hear the horn, the trumpet, sound so late — when it's useless and too late . . . Even on Monday our heads were still full of what kind of a service we should buy — whether to buy a Japanese or a Chinese one . . . So terribly important! But what's wrong with an ordinary tin mug? And what if we were to be given one more year to live wisely on condition we had to drink out of a mug like that?

ALDA

(*weeping*) Daddy! This is just an attack you're having! You're going to live! You're going to write again! And I'll help you, do you want me to? Something simple like copying scores, I can do that . . .

MAURICE

(*He strokes her head and caresses her. After a pause*) Why

123

is it you're so kind to me, my daughter? . . . You're the only one who never in her whole life demanded anything from me — no china services, no suites of furniture . . . My own darling! When I think what you used to wear in winter . . . How is it that I never even gave you a dress or had an overcoat made for you? (*They both weep.*)

ALDA

Let me go! I'll call a doctor! You're seriously ill!

MAURICE

No. They've worn me out. I want none of them! . . . Of all my relatives you are the only one to have music in your soul and it was you I wouldn't permit to study . . . Recently you came here to play and I didn't even find the time to listen to you . . . Heir of my soul! This piano is now yours, you hear? (*taking her head in his hands*) Will you ever forgive me, my daughter? . . . (*Alda puts her arms around him.*) Alda dear! Over there, look . . . (*pointing to one of the shelves*) Schubert. Get me the *Winterreise*. We'll play it together.

ALDA

Daddy! Something else! Not the *Winterreise*!

MAURICE

No, it must be the *Winterreise*! (pushing her) Hurry, or I'll never hear it again. A winter journey . . . (*Wiping away her tears, Alda looks around for the library steps, puts them against the bookshelves, and climbs up. Looking out of the window, Maurice talks to himself.*) If Schubert didn't flinch at the age of thirty — what do I have to be frightened of at the age of seventy? And what good is life to someone who does not know how to live? . . . In the middle of a snowstorm . . . a snowstorm . . . Everyone is able to stay inside today, but someone . . .

> I may not choose the season
> Of my departure hence,
> I will not stay to reason,
> But straight the march commence.*

ALDA

    (*coming down the library steps*) Here it is, Daddy.

MAURICE

    (*absentmindedly*) Good. Play. (*Alda switches on the light by the piano, sits down, and plays the Lied "Gute Nacht." Maurice sings very softly.*)

> A stranger I came hither,
> A stranger hence I go . . .

He is suddenly unable to sing any more and puts his hands to his chest. Alda continues to play, weeping.

---

* *Franz Schubert: Songs with Pianoforte Accompaniment*, English trans. Theo. Baker (New York: G. Schirmer, n.d.).

The original text by Wilhelm Müller of these lines from "Gute Nacht," the first song in Schubert's song-cycle *Die Winterreise* (*The Winter Journey*) is:

> Ich kann zu meiner Reisen
> Nicht wählen mit der Zeit;
> Muss selbst den Weg mir weisen
> In dieser Dunkelheit.
>
> Fremd bin ich eingezogen,
> Fremd zieh' ich wieder aus.
>
> Was soll ich länger weilen,
> Dass man mich trieb' hinaus?
> Lass irre Hunde heulen
> Vor ihres Herren Haus!
>
> Will dich im Traum nicht stören,
> Wär schad' um deine Ruh',
> Sollst meinen Tritt nicht hören —
> Sacht, sacht die Türe zu!

Solzhenitsyn uses the Russian version by S. Zayaitsky (which follows the German text fairly closely), except for the last section, which reads in literal translation, "It has long been time for me/ To throw my knapsack from my tired shoulders./ Long time for me to rest,/ Somewhere to lie down." (Translator.)

> Until they say: Begone here,
> Why do I longer wait?
> Let stray dogs bay the moon here
> Before her father's gate.

Alda continues to play while Maurice slowly lies down.

ALDA

(*singing alone*)

> Your sleep shall not be broken,
> Yet o'er your door I'll write,
> This simple farewell token,
> Goodnight, my dear, goodnight.

(*She goes on playing, then looks around in alarm, and breaks off.*) Daddy! Daddy!! . . . (*running to him*) Father! Are you alive?! (*shouting*) *Father!!* (*Shaking all over in anguish, she goes down on her knees and bends over the dying man.*)

Aunt Christine enters in ragged dark clothing, carrying a small bundle. She looks on silently from the door and then goes slowly over to the bed. Alda is sobbing. Christine uses a little mirror to test if the dead man is still breathing, then kisses his forehead, and makes the sign of the cross over him. She takes out the candle which she has brought with her, puts it at the head of the bed, and lights it. Meanwhile Alda falls silent. Aunt Christine opens a book and begins to read in a powerful voice.

AUNT CHRISTINE

"No man, when he hath lighted a candle, putteth it in a secret place, neither under a bushel, but on a candlestick, that they which come in may see the light."*

* The Scriptural texts are from Luke 11:33; 11:35; 12:19; and 12:20. (Translator.)

"Take heed therefore that the light which is in thee be not darkness." (*There is a pause while she turns over the page. Then she again begins to read solemnly.*)

"And I will say to my soul, Soul, thou hast much goods laid up for many years; take thine ease, eat, drink, and be merry." (*Tillie and Sinbar enter rapidly. After them comes Jim in a motorcycle helmet and gloves and wearing goggles. They all stop suddenly, leaning forward.*)

"But God said unto him, Thou fool, this night thy soul shall be required of thee: then whose shall those things be, which thou hast provided?"

Everyone remains motionless.

CURTAIN

SCENE SIX

A small, sparsely furnished room on the ground floor with two windows in the rear wall and a low door the same size as the windows. It is evidently evening and it is dark outside. There is a kitchen area in one corner. One can see a desk, a simple bed, and the same record player on a table and record cabinet as in Scene 1. The record player is open and there is a record on the turntable.

Alex is sitting at the desk. There is a light knock on the door and Alda enters carrying a parcel and a bunch of flowers.

ALDA

Hi, you old bear. Still sitting there? It's spring outside. Look what flowers they're selling.

ALEX

The flowers are nice. But it's enough to know that they're on sale. Why should one have to have them on one's table every day? It's monotonous.

ALDA

Flowers — monotonous?

ALEX

In any case it contradicts the principle of the economy of internal energy. Slave to death to earn a few ducats and then squander them. If there's one thing in particular you love, you have to sacrifice everything else for it.

128

ALDA

You ought to be glad that at least I still have a fondness for flowers. (*She buries her face in the flowers.*) After all I'm now a kind of half-person.

ALEX

(*going up to her*) Forgive me, Alda. I've been upset all this time and I don't know what I'm saying.

ALDA

What is it you say you love that you have to sacrifice everything else for?

ALEX

I don't understand it myself. I'm forty years old, I'm full of strength — and yet I'm just floundering. One thing's harmful. Another's useless. A third thing bores me to tears.

He sits down again with his head bowed. Alda takes off her raincoat; underneath she is wearing a black dress. She stands near the kitchen area.

ALDA

Nothing's changed here at all since last Saturday. If you think you can keep dirty saucepans and plates for months like this . . . And Aunt Christine can't tear herself away from her cats . . .

She takes a white apron out of her parcel, puts it on, and rolls up her sleeves.

ALEX

(*noticing what she is doing*) No, no, Alda! Don't do it! I don't want you to!

He hurries over to her and stops her before she has had time to finish tying the apron.

ALDA

Why not?

ALEX

I don't want you to bother with that.

ALDA

Me in particular? (*after a pause*) But I'm like a sister to you. (*after another pause*) All right, then I won't accept anything from you either.

ALEX

Listen, you can't compare the two things. If you start looking after everything here, that means essentially that . . .

ALDA

When you help me . . . or when you stop me from doing something . . . you always insist that you're my brother.

ALEX

When is it I stop you from doing anything?

ALDA

You stopped me from going to work in Philip's institute.

ALEX

(*heatedly*) But if you go and work there they won't be able to resist stabilizing you again. Your father's death saved you from that horror! Saved you from my terrible mistake. From my guilt towards you . . .

ALDA

You knew then better than me that I ought to agree . . . And now you know better than me that I ought not to . . . But what about my son — would you be able to bring him up better than I would? You wouldn't be able to bring up your own son, Al . . . because of your principle of the economy of energy. The best thing a son can have is a stabilized mother. (*She puts her head on his chest. There is a long pause.*)

ALEX

Did you take him to his father?

ALDA

Yes.

ALEX

What is it they want?

ALDA

I don't know what they want! . . . I don't know! . . .
(*She weeps on his chest.*)

ALEX

God, how everything is mixed up in this world, how complicated everything is! (*after a pause*) These gentlemen
who performed belated justice in quashing my conviction
— they really think that they have restored me to my former life . . . But everything has vanished. Who can now
revive the root of life I grew from? (*raising Alda's head*)
Who can return to me the girl I once knew, the girl I once
knew? . . .

*There is a crash on the other side of the wall as if something
had fallen. Alex and Alda move away from each other.
Alda wipes her eyes. Alex hurries to the door, but Philip
and Annie are already entering.*

PHILIP

We knocked something over, Alex old boy. But it was
empty. Oh, so Alda's here too?

ANNIE

We expected she would be, though. You didn't mess up
your suit? (*She examines Philip's suit.*)

PHILIP

(*also examining his suit*) No, it doesn't look like it. (*to
Alex*) Well? The runaway! Hello! (*He shakes his hand
with an energetic flourish.*) Hello, Alda. Hello, my silent
reproach! Our creation!

There are greetings all round.

ALEX

Ours, Phil?

PHILIP

Now — now — now — now! We've got everything under control. Our slight failure in Alda's case, just a partial failure, hasn't invalidated but only contributed to our system of neurostabilization. It's shown us what surprise developments we have to allow for. We'll need to use a different voltage frequency distribution and include extra series of treatments, but we're continuing our experiments on human beings — they promise to be enormously successful! And I believe that Alda will agree to come back.

ALEX

No, that's enough! You're not to touch Alda again.

ALDA

But why not? I felt so calm then.

PHILIP

Uh-huh? So you've really eaten her up? You tyrant! (*laughing*) So what are you up to? Listening to music? Some mournful dirge? (*The melodious theme from the first movement* (Allegro con brio) *of Beethoven's Second Piano Concerto is heard. They all listen for a short while.*) That's just what I was afraid of. Sheer dope. (*He takes the needle off the record.*) You don't have any Paraguayan dances, do you? They really get you fired up! Life is a struggle! (*Alda has meanwhile taken off her apron and put it back in the parcel. She and Annie sit down a little distance away.*) So that's how it is. So you're sitting here putting on one record after another — obviously Uncle Maurice gave you his collection. (*warmly*) Al! Come back to us!

ALEX

You'll be able to get on without me now.

PHILIP

What you're doing is called abandoning a friend.

ALEX

You mustn't abandon a friend when he's in trouble. But you can when he's at the summit of his success.

PHILIP

That's just it. That's precisely why I'm here.

ALEX

Thanks, Phil. But you see a person is unhappy only insofar as he's convinced of it himself.

PHILIP

But you just can't live this way. You're not earning anything.

ALEX

No, what do you mean — I'm still employed by the university, they pay me.

PHILIP

And how — just a pittance!

ALEX

It's not a question of how much you earn, it's a question of how little you spend. I only need half a ducat a day. I'm not saving to buy a car.

PHILIP

You have a difficult character. You'll never find a wife who could get along with you. Some people are involuntary failures. But you're a failure in accordance with a preconceived theory. Take science — you have no idea *what it's for*! You have talent — but you can see no purpose for it!

ALEX

No, I think I can see a purpose for it.

PHILIP

Well?

ALEX

I'll tell you, only don't laugh. You remember you once said that you felt like a relay runner — that you would be proud to hand on the baton of Great Physics to the twenty-first century?

PHILIP

Yes, I believe I did once.

ALEX

(*going up to the record player*) Well, I'd like to help pass on to the next century one particular baton — the flickering candle of our soul. (*He puts the needle back on the record and the main theme of the Rondo of the Beethoven concerto is softly heard. Alex indicates with his hand the way in which the melody successively quivers and runs on, then switches off the record player.*) Let them do whatever they want to it in the twenty-first century. Just so they don't blow it out in our century, in our century of steel and the atom, of space, electric power, and cybernetics . . .

PHILIP

(*puzzled*) And what are we supposed to do to achieve that, in practical terms?

ALEX

That's the problem . . .

ALDA

(*to Annie*) For two days she sobbed on my shoulder beside the coffin in front of the newspaper photographers and kept on shouting, "The poor little girl! I'll be like a father to her." But they'd scarcely filled in the grave when she started slandering me, calling me a thief and an intriguer, as if I were trying to appropriate Daddy's piano under false pretenses. But Daddy really did leave it to me.

134

My first childhood memories are of him sitting playing that piano. And it was on that piano that he started to teach me to play when I was a little girl . . . But Al tells me that it's a good thing I didn't get the piano in the end, it wouldn't have gone through the window or the door in my room.

ANNIE

How everything's changed in their house! The library and the manuscripts have been sold and Jim's been forced to go and work. Tillie got a terrible chewing-out from the Iron Captain for wrecking our work with you.

PHILIP

Sinbar is going to have his own independent institute now as well — a separate institute of Medical Cybernetics.

ALEX

Who's funding it? The same bosses?

PHILIP

What's bad about that? We have a very fruitful field of research.

ALEX

Too fruitful in fact! Eventually you'll get to be able to read human thoughts.

PHILIP

That's incredibly enticing! But thought turned out to be isoenergetic: correct and incorrect thoughts, affirmative and negative thoughts possess exactly the same energy, and it's impossible to distinguish between them.

ALEX

That's wonderful!

PHILIP

A real tragedy.

ALEX

But don't give up. You'll begin to figure out the shape of

the curve, I know! And one fine day you'll receive a visit from the gentlemen from the three-letter institution . . .

PHILIP

What three-letter institution?

ALEX

The DTF — the Department of Thoughts and Feelings. They'll put a guard around your computers and they'll start reading people's thoughts. But if that ever comes to pass — let it not be with any assistance on my part. In that event I would not only not want to work in your institute, I would not want to remain alive at all.

PHILIP

I don't know. So far we haven't got that far.

ALEX

"Lie detectors" exist already, the rest is not too far away.

PHILIP

But what about you? You! You've already tasted cybernetics, now you're infected and won't be able to give it up. What branch of cybernetics are you going to work in? Space cybernetics?

ALEX

We've lost nothing in Space. It's on earth that we are losing the last thing that still belongs to us.

PHILIP

Well then, social cybernetics, perhaps? (*with a boisterous laugh*) Joining Terbolm?

ALEX

Yes, look — I've had these two letters from him. He wants me to work for him.

PHILIP

But they don't have any backing at all or any funds, they're just a little clique, a soap bubble! (*He reads the letters.*)

136

ALEX

He sent me a tape-recorded letter as well. From the hospital. (*He puts the cassette on a tape recorder.*)

PHILIP

What, is he having trouble with his legs again? (*He continues to read, not listening to the recording.*)

TERBOLM'S VOICE

(*tape-recorded*) You were always asking, Coriel, *what* science was *for*? I'm back in bed again now and suddenly I've clearly realized the answer. There's no need to be worried about the extrinsic aims of science — who's directing it and in what direction, what practical use is going to be made of it. In fact, many times people have harnessed it to go one way, and it's just laughed and pulled a different way. But apart from the obvious aims which are visible to everyone, science has concealed aims as well. Like art. Science is needed not only by our intellect, but also by our soul. Perhaps it's just as necessary for us to understand the world and to understand mankind as it is to . . . have a conscience! Yes, that's my hypothesis: we need science also as a conscience! (*pause*) But now (*Philip is still reading. Alex looks at him intently.*) . . . they are going to give the microphone . . .

ALEX

(*abruptly stopping the tape recorder*) The rest isn't important.

ANNIE

(*to Alda*) Living with me, he's always cheerful and full of energy. Doesn't the very fact of our happiness together justify us? . . . And we've put her in the best hospital we could find.

PHILIP

(*giving back the letters*) Ha — ha — ha! They're a com-

137

pletely disreputable outfit! "Algorithms for an ideally regulated society"! — but where are we to get these algorithms from if no genius has dreamed them up yet? No, tell me, you brute, in what way do you find this field superior to ours?

ALEX

It does have some advantages.

PHILIP

What advantages? !

ALEX

I see it this way: biocybernetics means interfering with the most perfect thing that exists on earth — man! Why? ? ! On the other hand social cybernetics dares to introduce reason where before there had been eternal chaos and injustice, to interfere with the most *imperfect* of earthly organizations — human society.

PHILIP

What is this then exactly? Cybernetic socialism?

ALEX

Terbolm swears that it's even better than socialism.

PHILIP

But it's nonsense! Charlatanism! Terbolm's a fanatic. Nor does he have any fighting qualities, the drive to come out on top.

ALEX

Well I'll try to contribute them.

PHILIP

Then there's the matter of elementary prudence: how about the state? You'll all get your heads chopped off, have you really forgotten Caledonia already?

ALEX

That's precisely my advantage over you: since I have nothing, there is nothing I am afraid of losing. I'm so

138

glad that you and I have had this talk! It's this conversation that's made me understand: I'm going to join them! It's my duty to join them!

PHILIP

Watch out! In the hope of success . . .

ALEX

In the hope? No! You didn't understand. Not in hope, but in terror! In fear of success! I'm going to join them in order to prevent their eventually becoming another Leviathan, this time an electronic Leviathan.

PHILIP

(*coldly*) *So*? . . . Well, watch out. Watch out.

ALEX

(*putting one hand on Philip's shoulder, speaking in a tone of profound affection*) I've been watching *you*, Phil! All these months. And I've been wanting to tell you for a long time that . . .
The sound of a long hoot on a car horn somewhere nearby is heard.

ANNIE

(*to Philip*) We must go.

ALEX

They're calling you.

PHILIP

(*getting up*) Yes . . . (*The women also get up. There is a pause. All stand.*) Nevertheless, Al, I don't believe you're completely lost yet.

ALEX

I even believe that you're not either. Not completely.
Alda meanwhile has picked up her raincoat.

PHILIP

Well, all right, just don't stop me from talking to Alda. She's about to leave and we'll see her off.

ALEX

> (*making a movement to restrain Alda*) Alda's only just come. She's not going . . .

ALDA

> (*freeing herself*) No, no, Al, I have to go.

PHILIP

> (*helping Alda into her raincoat*) Stop making decisions for other people! Don't you realize I'm in a position to offer Alda a good job? A — good — job?

ALEX

> But *that's* not what's important, surely? Alda!

ALDA

> But what is important then? Surely *you* don't know what's important?
>
> *Alda leaves with Annie. Philip pats his friend on the shoulder and leaves also. Alex stands in the middle of the room with his head bowed.*
>
> *The light goes out. Then suddenly the back of the room is radiantly illuminated by the bright headlights of a car facing the window. Alex runs to the window and opens it wide. The car is evidently turning around in the street. Then with its engine roaring the car moves past the window so that its headlights sweep across the room. The back of the room nevertheless remains radiantly illuminated, since now a second car repeats the maneuver of the first and drives past with its headlights sweeping the room to the accompaniment of the same roar from its superb engine.*

ALEX

> A-ha, so they didn't come alone! "Mottled Burgundy"! Tillie and Sinbar were here too. Ships of the blessed! . . .
> *The light comes on again. Alex goes dejectedly over to the tape recorder and restarts the tape.*

But now they are going to give the microphone to Nika.
She also wants to say something to you.

NIKA'S VOICE

Alex! Since Philip brought me here in the winter he hasn't
come to visit me once. And I thought to myself: what if he
is torturing himself? What if he is simply afraid of exacer-
bating my suffering with his healthy appearance and his
happiness — and doesn't come just for that reason? Then
give him this tape recording.

Philip! Philip! ! I know that I will never get up again. And
don't you be ashamed, live your own life. Conquer! . . .
And love — whoever you want. I won't reproach you . . .
But once . . . in spring. And once in summer. And once
in autumn — come to see me, don't be embarrassed. Sit
with me for an hour. And talk to me as if everything had
stayed the same . . . What will it cost you, Philip? ! !

(*pause*) Alex! But if it's for a different reason that he
doesn't come — he's not to listen to this tape . . .

*Alex stands despondently. In the distance the earlier melo-
dy from* Die Winterreise *played on a single horn can be
faintly heard. Alex does not notice the mournful figure of
Alda, dressed in black, appear outside the window. With
lowered head she walks past the closed first window very
slowly, then stops at the second window, which is open,
and sadly looks inside. After this she walks away, still
with her head lowered, remaining indistinctly visible for
some time in the light of a streetlamp.*

CURTAIN